India of Mahatma Gandhi's Dreams
Miles Away

Sheshrao Chavan

ATLANTIC
PUBLISHERS & DISTRIBUTORS (P) LTD

Published by
ATLANTIC
PUBLISHERS & DISTRIBUTORS (P) LTD
7/22, Ansari Road, Darya Ganj, New Delhi-110002
Phones : +91-11-40775252, 40775214, 23273880, 23275880
Fax : +91-11-23285873
Web : www.atlanticbooks.com
E-mail : orders@atlanticbooks.com

Branch Office: Chennai
Phones : +91-44-48531784, 28291383
E-mail : chennai@atlanticbooks.com

Printed & bound in India by Atlantic Print Services

Preface

Mahatma Gandhi returned to India in January 1915 from South Africa with the determination to free India from British Yoke. The very first thing he did after returning to India was to call on Gopal Krishna Gokhale whom he had accepted as his Guru.

Gokhale advised Gandhi to spend first year in India with his eyes and ears open but mouth shut. During those twelve months, Gandhi travelled in India; assessed the situation and the miserable plight in which masses were living. He was convinced that India must get rid of the British overlords. He gathered Sardar Patal, Jawaharlal Nehru, and like them around him and formulated a plan of action, the beginning of which he made from his native state Gujarat by launching 'Dandi March', which came to be known as 'Salt Satyagraha'. When Gandhi reached the sea at Dandi, his small ashram band had grown into a non-violent army of several thousand strong. He dipped into the water, returned to the beach, and there picked up some salt left by the waves. Smt. Sarojini Naidu who was standing by his side shouted, "Hail Deliverer".

Subhash Chandra Bose compared the 'Dandi March' to Nepoleon's March to Paris on his return from Elba. The whole nation was stirred. More than 60,000 political offenders were arrested.

Every movement of Gandhi, thereafter, led to shaking the British Empire. He went on fast for one day, seven days, 21 days, and fast unto death on several occasions. But, nothing deterred him. At times, it appeared that he is passing away, but he had unflinching faith in God. He said, "He (God) will not take him away until the goal is achieved". And the goal was achieved on 15th August 1947.

The Independence Day was being celebrated with all pomp and show in Delhi, but Gandhi was in Calcutta exerting to restore peace in the strife-torn city.

Anand Shankar Ray, in his book, "Yes, I saw Gandhi" on page 6 and 7 writes: "What happened in Calcutta on 15th of August 1947 was uncanny. One man had the power to bring it about—Gandhi. The tragedy of the Punjab was on the point of being re-enacted. Floods of people fleeing for their lives would have poured into India in the wake of rivers of blood streaming from Dacca to Calcutta, swamping the whole of Bengal. That a tragedy of that magnitude was prevented by the influence of a single man was a fact to be recorded on the pages of history in letters of gold. Could he have done it if he had not been *advesta sarva bhutanam maitra karunah?* Or his non-violent technique had not been adequate? It was true. Yes true. It happened.

If Gandhi had not waved his magic wand, the holocaust of the Punjab would have been repeated in Bengal. There is little doubt about it."

Lord Mountbatten paid finest tribute to Gandhi for his work in Calcutta and Noakhali through his letter of 26th August 1947 in which he said:

> In the Punjab, we have 55,000 soldiers and large scale rioting on our hands. In Bengal our forces consisted of one man, and there is no rioting. As a serving officer as well as an administrator, may I be allowed to pay my tribute to the One Man Boundary Force.

Delhi—A City of Dead

No sooner Gandhi's fast restored Calcutta to its senses and peace, the news came that Delhi was on fire. He returned to Delhi on 9th September 1947. Sardar Patel received him at Shahadara Railway Station and briefed him on the situation prevailing in Delhi, which had become the city of the dead.

Gandhi issued a statement to the press, in which he said, "I must apply the old formula, "Do or Die" and he went on fast on 13th January 1948 with an announcement that he would break his fast only when Delhi became peaceful in the real sense of the term". He laid down seven conditions to break his fast, which were accepted by the leaders of all parties. Thereafter, Gandhi ended his fast. After ending the fast, he said, "If the pledge was kept, it would revive his will to live for full span of 125 years". But, it was not to be. Nathuram Godse—a Brahamin from Poona, an editor of a Marathi newspaper, and a member of the Hindu Mahasabha—shot him dead on 30th January 1948, while he was going for his daily prayer meeting at the lawns of Birla House.

Although his violent end was ironical, still Smt. Sarojini Naidu could say of it, "This was the only death great enough for him". Never in modern history has any man been mourned more deeply and more widely as Gandhi. The Government of India received 3441 messages of sympathy, all unsolicited from foreign countries as given in chapter 8.

Mind-set Behind Gandhi's Assassination

The mind-set behind Gandhi's assassination has been described in Chapter–7. Shri Dhiru S. Mehta in his Foreword to my book, *Last Days of Mahatma Gandhi*, says, "The death of Gandhiji brought existence a philosophy which is not only the basis of state craft in India, but influenced people all over the world".

India of Mahatma Gandhi's Dreams—Miles Away

Gandhi wanted to build India of his dreams as detailed in Chapter–9. But the Congress, in spite of ruling India for the major period after independence, did not proceed in that direction. Jawaharlal Nehru, in his zeal and enthusiasm to follow Fabian Socialism, went for Public Sector undertakings and construction of big dams like Bhakra-Nangal. However, having disillusioned, in the evening of his life, he admitted that he should have gone to Gandhian way. His successors also did not pay heed to Gandhian ways. The cumulative result of all these is the plight in which India is placed.

In case India is to be brought out of the clutches of three Ms i.e. Money power, Mafia power, and Muscle power and the democracy is to be made in the real sense of the term "Government of the people, for the people, and by the people" instead of "Government off the people, buy the people, and far the people", good citizens who are in large number, will have to enter public and social life to overthrow evils obtaining. They must recollect what Sri Aurobindo said and I quote, "If good people keep away from public life, goondas will dominate it". They should also recollect what Plato said, "The punishment suffered by the wise men, who refuse to take part in Government is to live under the Government of bad men". Edmund Burk said, "All that is necessary for the triumph of evil is that good men do nothing". Danial Webster said, "Nothing will ruin the country, if the people themselves will undertake its safety; and nothing can save it, if they leave that safety in any hands but theirs".

I hope wisdom will dawn on good people to rise before it becomes further late.

What Gandhi said about India of his dreams as given in detail in Chapter–9 stands true even today—may it be villages, agriculture, rural and urban sanitation, and village health.

Gandhi explained in detail the evil wrought by the foreign medium. He went to the extent of saying, "If I had the powers of a despot, I would stop the tuition of our boys and girls through foreign medium and require all the teachers and professors on pain of dismissal to introduce the change forthwith".

Today, there is a mad race to impart teaching through English medium from KG to PG. in villages as well as cities without bothering to know the knowledge assimilated by the students. And all this is not for academic purpose but for minting money.

In sum, it can be said that India of Mahatma Gandhi's Dreams is miles away.

Ray of Hope

One may or may not agree, but I see that Prime Minister Narendra Modi's programs under Swachhata Abhiyan for rural and urban sanitation, skill development programmes for self-employment, massive electrification of villages and towns, schemes for welfare of farmers, and encouragement for use of swadeshi and Khadi may lead to build India of Mahatma Gandhi's Dreams. But, let me hasten to say that it would be premature to draw conclusion.

Sheshrao Chavan

Contents

1
India Becomes Independent

At midnight on 14th August 1947, the curtain came down on 'British Raj' in India. The moment was marked by a stirring ceremony in the Central Hall of the Parliament. The high point of ceremony was lyrical speech by Pandit Jawaharlal Nehru. He began "Long years ago, we made a tryst with destiny, and now the time comes when we shall redeem our pledge, not wholly or in full measure, but very substantially. At the stroke of the mid-night hour, when the world sleeps, India will awake to life and freedom. A moment comes, which comes but rarely in history when we step out from the old to the new, when an age ends, and when the soul of a nation, long suppressed finds utterance. It is fitting that at this solemn moment we take the pledge of dedication to the service of India and her people and to the still larger cause of humanity", and he ended by saying "This is no time for petty and destructive criticism, no time for ill will or blaming others. We have to build the noble mansion of free India where all her children may dwell."

Calcutta Killings

Gandhiji had no desire to be in Delhi when independence was declared. He, therefore, took a train straight from Lahore to Patna, from where he intended to proceed to Noakhali via Calcutta. He stopped at Patna on August 8, and advised the people of Bihar to spend the day of independence in prayer, fasting and spinning. The next day Gandhiji arrived in Calcutta.

Gandhiji's stay in Calcutta was to have been brief. At Sodepur Ashram, the Chief Minister of the newly formed cabinet for West Bengal and the leader of the West Bengal Assembly Congress Party P.C. Ghosh, met Gandhiji to tell him about the situation in the city. Governor Fredrick Burrows, also invited him to discuss Calcutta.

On August 10, a large Muslim deputation met Gandhiji to appeal to him to stay in Calcutta saying 'We Muslims have as much claim upon you as the Hindus.' For you yourself have said 'you are as much of Muslims as of Hindus'.

Suhrawardy, who was no longer premier, also begged Gandhiji to pacify Calcutta before proceeding to Noakhali. Gandhiji told Suhrawardy and other Muslim leaders that if he agreed to stay in Calcutta, it would be on two conditions.

Suhrawardy and other league leaders will have to extract from the Muslims of Noakhali a solemn pledge of the safety of the Hindus in their midst. If a single Hindu was killed, he (Gandhi) would have no choice but to fast to death.

Suhrawardy will have to live with him (Gandhiji) day and night, side by side unarmed and unprotected.

Suhrawardy and others agreed to both the conditions. On August 13, Gandhiji shifted from Sodepur to Baliaghat, one of the most sensitive and overcrowded spots of the city, strife-torn, congested and filthy, with a mixed population of rival communities, already prepared for killing each other. There, inside ruined and deserted Muslim house known as Hydari Mansion. Gandhiji fixed his abode to wait for the dawn of independence. "I have got stuck up here and I am now going to undertake a grave risk. Suhrawardy and I are going from today to stay together in a Muslim quarter. The future will reveal itself", he informed Sardar Patel. Patel wrote back:

> So you have got detained in Calcutta and that too in a quarter which is a veritable shambles and a notorious

> den of gangsters and hooligans. And in what choice company too! It is a terrible risk. But more than that, will your health stand the strain? I am afraid, it must be terribly filthy there. Keep me posted about yourself.

Gandhiji arrived at the Hydari Mansion in his old pre-war Chevrolet car in the afternoon of August 13. The Police Commissioner came there and told Gandhiji he does not have enough police force to protect him.

Hydari Mansion, an old abandoned Muslim house in an indescribably filthy locality, had hastily been cleared up for Gandhiji's residence. It was a ramshackle building open on all sides to the crowds. Before many days all the glass in windows was smashed. There was only one latrine and it was used indiscriminately by hundreds of people, including the police on duty, the visitors and even the darshan-seeking crowd. One room was reserved for Gandhiji. Another had been set apart for his luggage, and the members of his party, and the guests. A third served as his office.

The people upon whom Gandhiji had to work were already waiting for him. They were all Hindus and many of them had seen their relatives butchered, wives and daughters raped by the Muslim mobs of the Direct Action Day. They began cursing Gandhiji instead of cheering 'Save Hindus not Muslims'. And 'Traitor to the Hindus'. They showered the car with stones.

Raising his hand in a gesture of peace. Gandhiji walked alone into the shower of stones and began to reason with them: "I was on my way to Noakhali where your own kith and kin desired my presence. But I now see that I shall have to serve Noakhali only from here. You must understand that I have come here to serve not only Muslims but Hindus, Muslims and all alike. Those who are indulging in brutalities are bringing disgrace upon themselves and the religion they represent. I am going to put myself under your protection. You are welcome to turn against me and play the opposite role if you so choose. I have nearly reached the end of my life's journey. I have much farther to go. But let me tell you, if you again go mad, I will not be a living witness to it. I have given the same ultimatum to the Muslims of Noakhali also. I have earned the right. Before there is another outbreak of Muslim madness in Noakhali, they will find me dead."

"How can I, who am a Hindu by birth, a Hindu by deed, a Hindu of Hindu in my way of living, be an enemy of the Hindus?" he asked the angry crowd.

Gandhiji's reasoning and the simplicity of his approach puzzled and disturbed the crowd. Promising to talk further, he and his followers entered the Hydari Mansion.

On further dialogue, the young men were completely won over. They undertook to do all in their power to win over their friends to work with Gandhiji for peace and goodwill. Said one of them afterwards to another. "What a spell-binder this old man is! No matter how heavy the odds, he does not know what defeat is!" Some of them later guarded his house as volunteers when armed guards were withdrawn after the 15th August.

Thus Calcutta quickly came under the spell of the Mahatma and changed its explosive character rather dramatically and quite unexpectedly. As countless men, women of all persuasions continued to make their pilgrimage to the Hydari Mansion, anger and excitement started dying down, yielding to a new spirit of fraternity that came to prevail. On August 14, Gandhiji said to his evening prayer congregation, which must have been over a lakh people.

"From tomorrow we shall be delivered from the bondage of the British rule. But from midnight today, India will be partitioned too. While, therefore, tomorrow will be a day of rejoicing, it will be a day of sorrow as well. It will throw a heavy burden of responsibility upon us. Let us pray to God that He may give us strength to bear it worthily. Let all those Muslims who were forced to flee return their homes. If two millions of Hindus and Muslims are at daggers drawn with one another in Calcutta, with what face can I go to Noakhali and plead the cause of the Hindus with the Muslims there? And if the flames of communal strife envelop the whole country how can our new born freedom survive?"

Men, women and children in their thousands were waiting for his darshan as he went out for his morning walk. Eager crowd besieged the mansion the whole day. Every half an hour he had to come out to give darshan. The members of the West Bengal cabinet also came for his blessings. Gandhiji said to them: "From today you have to wear the crown of thorns. Strive ceaselessly to cultivate truth and non-violence. Be humble. Be forbearing. The British rule no doubt put you on your mettle. But now you will be tested through and through. Beware of power; power corrupts. Do not let yourselves be entrapped by its pomp and pageantry. Remember, you are in office to serve the poor in India's villages. May God help you." It was unpalatable advice, but it was given in all seriousness.

Stirring scenes of national rejoicing marked by unique demonstrations of Hindu-Muslim unity were witnessed in Calcutta on the 15th August. From early morning mixed parties Hindus and Muslims began to go about in trucks in various parts of the city shouting slogans. "Hindu Muslim Ek Ho" (Let Hindus and Muslims unite) and "Hindu Muslim Bhai Bhai" (Hindus and Muslims are brothers). It was as if the black clouds of a year's of madness the sunshine of sanity and goodwill had suddenly broken through.

Nearly 30,000 persons gathered that evening in the prayer ground. Gandhiji congratulated the citizens of Calcutta on the unity they had achieved. If the delirious fraternization in the city was sincere and not momentary, it was better even than in the Khilafat days. He said.

Following Gandhiji, Suhrawardy addressed the gathering. Until the Hindus went back to their abandoned homes and the Muslims to theirs, they would not think, he said that their work was finished. Some people thought, he continued, that Hindu-Muslim unity could never be achieved but by God's will and Mahatmaji's *Kripa* (grace) what only three or four days before was considered and impossibility has miraculously turned into a fact.

Rajaji came to see Gandhiji in the course of the day. As a mark of respect he left his sandals at the entrance, and walked the whole length of the hall barefoot.

On August 17, a large multitude of men and women from all communities had been waiting for Gandhiji at the square of Narikeldonga. Addressing the gathering, he said, "Everybody is showering congratulations on me for the miracle Calcutta is witnessing. Let us all thank God for His abundant mercy, but let us not forget that there are isolated spots in Calcutta where all is not well." He asked his followers—Hindus and Muslims alike to join him in prayer that the miracle of Calcutta would not prove to be momentary ebullition.

On the Islamic festival of Id, half a million of Hindus and Muslims gathered for Gandhiji's evening prayer on Calcutta's cricket ground. As it was Monday—his day of silence—Gandhiji spent much of the day in scrawling for his visitors little notes of gratitude and good wishes. As he did so, thousands of Hindus and Muslims paraded together through the streets. They chanted slogans of unity and friendship, sprayed each other with rose water, exchanged sweets and cakes.

At precisely seven o' clock in the evening visibly moved by the fabulous spectacle of so much love and brotherhood, shimmering before him, Gandhiji rose and joined his hands in the traditional Indian sign of greeting the crowd. Then he broke his silence to say, 'IdMubarak' (Happy Id).

The happenings in Calcutta had by now begun to radiate their influence in other parts of the country besides Bihar. On the 24th August, the Muslim League party in the Constituent Assembly of the Indian Union passed a resolution expressing its deep sense of appreciation of the services rendered by Mahatma Gandhi to the cause of restoration of peace and goodwill between the communities in Calcutta and saving hundreds of innocent lives and property from destruction.

In an article captioned, 'Miracle or Accident' in Harijan Gandhiji wrote:

> Shaheed Suhrawardy and I are living together in Beliaghat where Muslims have been reported to be sufferers. We are living in a Muslim house and Muslim volunteers are attending to our comforts with the greatest attention.... Here in the compound numberless Hindus and Muslims continue to stream in shouting the favourite slogans. One might almost say that the joy of fraternization is leaping up from hour to hour.

Is this to be called a miracle or an accident? By whatever name it may be described, it is quite clear that the credit that is being given to me from all sides is quite undeserved; nor can it be said to be deserved by Shaheed.... This sudden upheaval is not the work of one or two men. We are toys in the hands of God. He makes us dance to His tune. The utmost, therefore, that man can do is to refrain from interfering with the dance and that he should tender full obedience to his Maker's will. Thus considered, it can be said that in this miracle, He only ask whether the dream of my youth is to be realized in the evening of my life.

For those who have full faith in God, this is neither a miracle nor an accident. A chain of events can be clearly seen to show that the two were being prepared unconsciously to themselves, for fraternization. In this process our advent on the scene enabled the onlooker to give us credit for the consummation of the happy event.

But that as it may, the delirious happenings remind me of the early days of the Khilafat and Swaraj as our twin goals. Today we have nothing of the kind. We have drunk the position of mutual hatred and so this nectar of fraternization tastes all the sweeter and the sweetness should never wear out.

Wrote Lord Mountbatten to Gandhiji: "In the Punjab we have 55,000 soldiers and large-scale rioting on our hands. In Bengal our forces consist of one man, and there is no rioting. As a serving officer, as well as an administrator, may I be allowed to pay my tribute to the One-Man Boundary Force, not forgetting his Second in Command, Mr. Suhrawardy."

In reply Gandhiji wrote: "I do not know if Shaheed and I can legitimately appropriate the complement you pay us. Probably suitable conditions were ready for us to take the credit for what appears to have been a magical performance. Am I right in gathering from your letter that you would like me to try the same thing for the Punjab?"

'Gandhiji has achieved many things,' commented Rajagopalachari, 'but there has been nothing which is so truly wonderful as his victory over evil in Calcutta'.

Last But One Fast

The atmosphere of amity in Calcutta was, however, very short-lived. As reports of fresh happenings poured in from the Punjab, rioting again broke out. A transfer of population which Gandhiji and other leaders wanted to avoid took place automatically in the case of the Punjab, and the Frontier and Sind on account of fresh riots.

Exactly after sixteen miraculous days, at ten in the night of August 31, young Hindu fanatics burst into the court of Hydari Mansion, demanding to see Gandhiji. They began to shout the slogans and hurl stones at the Mansion. Manu and Abha woke up and rushed to the veranda trying to calm the crowd, but the crowd spilled into the interior of the Mansion. Gandhi aroused by the shouts got up to face them. "What madness is this, he asked, I offer myself for attack." However, his words were drowned in a violent din; a brick flew past him; a Lathi blow just missed him. Calcutta relapsed into rioting.

Pyarelal writes:

> Charu Chowdhary and myself, fearing a very serious reaction in Noakhali if the Calcutta situation deteriorated further, decided, on our own, to approach Hindu Mahasabha leaders and plead with them for their co-operation in Gandhiji's and Suhrawardy's peace effort.
>
> We saw Dr. Shyama Prasad Mookerjee first. He was suffering from acute gall-bladder trouble and had been ordered complete rest in bed. We told him that if the minority community in Noakhali or for that matter in the whole of East Bengal, was not to be exposed to an incalculable risk, the situation in Calcutta would have to be immediately brought under control. He listened to us with the greatest attention. At the end he said, "I shall certainly issue an appeal and do anything beside that you might suggest". He asked us to come after an hour when he would be ready with his statement. He proved as good as his word.
>
> When we returned to Hydari Mansion we found Gandhiji writing a letter to Dr. Mookerjee to ask whether it was not time that he issued an appeal to the Hindus of Calcutta. His face lit up as I handed him Dr. Mookerjee's draft statement. With some minor changes it was released to the press the next day.

'The continuance of peaceful conditions in West Bengal and East Bengal is essential for peace in India. Calcutta is the key to the situation. If it is at peace, it must influence East Bengal. Peace in the whole of Bengal must again affect the whole of the Punjab.... The majority community in Bengal must realize, the senseless oppression of innocent members of the minority community does not pay and creates a vicious circle which one cannot cut through. The united efforts of leaders of the communities must see to this'.

Pyarelal further writes:

> At about two in the afternoon news came that, a violent communal conflagration had broken out simultaneously in several parts of the city. Every ten minutes, fresh reports of incidents kept pouring in and with every fresh report deeper grew Gandhiji's self-introspection. He used to have drink of fruit juice in the afternoon. That day when it was brought to him, he waved it away.
>
> The day's news had created panic among the poorer Muslim inhabitants of Beliaghata who, on the strength of Gandhiji's previous assurance, had already returned to their homes. A batch of them boarded an open truck to go to the nearest Muslim locality. As the truck carrying them passed by the side of graveyard near Gandhiji's residence, hand-grenades were hurled upon it from the roof of an adjoining building and two Muslims were instantaneously killed.
>
> As soon as Gandhiji heard of the incident, he expressed a desire to go and see the victims, it was a piteous sight. The dead men lay in a pool of blood, their eyes glazed and swarm of flies buzzing over their wounds. They must have been poor day-labourers. One of them was clad in a tattered dhoti, A four anna piece, which he carried on his person, had rolled out of his cloth and lay at the sight of this cold-blooded butchery of innocent men. While returning to his residence someone asked Gandhiji if he was contemplating a fast.
>
> 'You are right,' he replied. 'I am praying for light. May be by nightfall I shall get a clear indication'. (*Mahatma Gandhi: The Last Phase Part II,* pp. 405-06)

The evening prayer was held within doors. The hymn sung at the prayer was: "No-one has ever been known to be disgraced while walking the way of the Lord". The prayer was still in progress when Shaheed Suhrawardy with N.C. Chatterji and several leading Marwari businessmen came in. They all admitted that the Hindus had completely lost their heads.

After the visitors had left. Gandhiji went out for his usual evening walk. Before he returned to the house he knew what he should do. He sat down to draft the statement embodying his decision.

When Rajaji came in at 10 p.m. Gandhiji showed him his draft. Glancing through it Rajaji, remarked, 'You do not expect me to approve of your proposed step'. Together they took stock of the situation and thrashed threadbare the issues at stake.

It was past eleven when Rajaji left with the final statement. It was released to the press the same night. After referring to the disturbances at Hydari Mansion on the night of 31st August, it went on:

> What is the lesson of the incident? It is clear to me that if India is to retain her dearly-won independence, all men and women must completely forget lynch law. What was attempted was an indifferent limitation of it. There is no way of keeping the peace in Calcutta or, elsewhere, if the elementary rule of civilized society is not observed.... The recognition of the golden rule of never taking the law into one's own hands has no exceptions....
>
> From the very day of the peace, that is August 14th last, I have been saying that the peace might only be a temporary lull. There was no miracle. Will the foreboding prove true and will Calcutta again lapse into the law of jungle? Let us hope not, let us pray to the Almighty that He will touch our hearts and ward off the recurrence of insanity.
>
> Since the foregoing was written...some of the places which were safe till yesterday (31st August) have

> suddenly become unsafe. Several deaths have taken place. I saw two bodies of very poor Muslims. I saw also some wretched-looking Muslims being carted away to a place of safety. I quite see the last night's incidents, so fully described above, pale into insignificance before this flare up. Nothing that I may do in the way of going about in the open conflagration could possibly arrest it.
>
> I have told the friends who saw me.... What their duty is. What part am I to play in order to stop it? The Sikhs and the Hindus must not forget what the East Punjab has done during these few days. Now the Muslims said that the Sikhs and the Hindus (of Calcutta) are enraged over the Punjab happenings.

'Now that the Calcutta bubble seems to have burst, with what face can I go to the Punjab? The weapon which has hitherto proved infallible for me is fasting. To put an appearance before a yelling crowd does not always work'. It did not certainly last night. What my word in person cannot do, my fast may. It may touch the hearts of all the warring elements in the Punjab if it does in Calcutta. I, therefore, begin fasting from 8.15 tonight to end only if and when sanity returns to Calcutta. I shall, as usual permit myself to add salt and soda to the water I may wish to drink during the fast.

'If the people of Calcutta wish me to proceed to the Punjab and help the people there, they have to enable me to break the fast as early as may be'.

Gandhiji woke up Abha and Manu and told them 'that as from 8.15 that evening his fast had commenced. It would terminate only when the disturbances would cease. It will be do or die. Either there will be peace or I shall be dead'.

In a few hours the news of Gandhiji's fast spread like a wild fire in the city. Hindu and Muslim leaders rushed to Gandhiji to beg him to give up his fast. One Muslim threw himself at his feet, crying. 'If anything happens to you, it will be the end for Muslims.' I will not break the fast until the glorious peace of the last fifteen days has been restored, Gandhiji made it clear.

Just then an appeal signed by some 40 representatives of the Hindu and Muslim residents of Narkeldonga. Sitaltala, Maniktola and Kankurgachi areas was brought in. The signatories pledged themselves that they would not allow any untoward incident to happen in those localities—the worst affected during the previous riots. They also reported for his information, that no incident occurred in these mixed areas since the 14th August 1947. They earnestly prayed to Gandhiji to break his fast.

The leaders then retired to the next room for consultation and remained there for nearly half an hour. The deliberations were brief but unhurried. Rajaji dictated the draft of the pledge which was signed first by N.C. Chatterji and D.N. Mukherji of the Hindu Mahasabha, followed by Shaheed Suhrawardy as the leader of the Muslim League Parliamentary Party of West Bengal. R.K. Jaidka, the Punjabi leader and Niranjan Singh Talib, the Sikh leader. Without any further loss of time the signatories returned to Gandhiji.

The document ran: "We the undersigned promise to Gandhiji that now that peace and quiet have been restored to Calcutta once again, we shall never allow communal strife in the city and shall strive unto death to prevent it."

Before breaking the fast, Gandhiji addressed a few words to the gathering in Hindustani: "I am breaking this fast so that I might be able to do something for the Punjab. I have accepted your assurance on its face value. I hope and pray I shall never have to regret it. I would certainly like to live to serve India and humanity, but I do not wish to be duped into prolonging my life. I hope I will not have again fast for the peace of Calcutta. Let me therefore warn you that you dare not relax your vigilance. Calcutta today holds the key to the peace of the whole of India. If something happens here, its repercussion, is bound to be felt, elsewhere. You should, therefore, solemnly resolve that even if the whole world went up in a blaze, Calcutta would remain untouched by the flames. You have just heard the song Ishwar and Allah are Thy names. May He be witness between you and me."

Seventy-three hours after it was commenced Gandhiji broke the fast at 9.15 p.m. on the 4th September by slowly sipping a glass of diluted orange juice. It was preceded by a short prayer, in which all present joined, followed the singing of Tagore's song:

> When the heart is hard and parched up,
> Come upon me with a shower of mercy

On the 7th September, Gandhiji's last day in Calcutta, at half past eight at night, some ladies came to bid him farewell by performing arti—centuries old ceremonial Hindu way of expressing devotion.

At 9 p.m. he boarded the train for Delhi at Belur—a way side station—where he was taken to avoid the crowds at the Howrah station. Among those who saw him off were the Chief Minister of Bengal with his fellow—Ministers and Shaheed Suhrawardy. Reverentially they took leave one after another. As the train started Suhrawardy's eyes were seen wet with tears—perhaps for the first time in his life in public.

2

Delhi—The City of Dead

Gandhiji arrived at Shahadara railway station of Delhi on September 9. He was received at the station by Sardar Patel, and taken to Birla House as the Bhangi Colony where he usually stayed was over crowded with refugees from Pakistan. Sardar briefed Gandhiji on the situation prevailing in Delhi, which had become the city of the dead.

Hardly Gandhiji's car arrived at Birla House when Pandit Nehru's drove up. As he gave Gandhiji news, his face was pinched and furrowed by care, overstrained and lack of sleep. A twenty-four hour curfew was in force in the city. The military had been called but firing and looting had not stopped altogether. The streets were littered with the dead. Nehru was indignant.

Under a notification issued by the Government of India. Delhi province was declared a dangerously disturbed area. Orders were issued to the police and the armed forces to shoot to kill law breakers. The notification permitted the infliction of death penalty for offences like attempt to murder, kidnapping, abduction, arson, dacoity and looting.

The biggest migration of population in recorded history was in progress. Almost ten million people were on move in both directions across the border in the Punjab. The Government had not anticipated an outbreak of such dimensions. The civil authority in both the Punjab was paralysed.

A military evacuation organization had been set up by the Indian Union Government which took over the evacuation of refugees from the civil authorities in the first week of September. All modes of transport were employed for the purpose—trains, motor cars and air planes. Between 27th August and 6th November, 673 trains carried 2,799,000 refugees inside India and across the border. Over 427,000 non-Muslims and over 217,000 Muslims were moved during the same period by motor transport using 1200 military and civil vehicles. 27000 evacuees were brought to India by Government chartered planes in 962 flights between 15th September and 7th December.

Mountbatten's remark in the Emergency Committee, 'If we go down in Delhi, we are finished' gave a true measure of gravity of the crisis with which the government were faced.

All eyes were turned on Gandhiji. But his own were turned inward. At last he spoke to the assembled leaders, Delhi was not Calcutta, he declared. "I find no one in Delhi who can accompany me and control the Muslims. There is no such person amongst the Sikhs or among the Rashtriya Swayam Sevak Sangh either. I do not know what I shall be able to do here. But one thing is clear, I cannot leave this place until Delhi is peaceful again."

He appeared to be buried in deep thought, 'God, Thou art my only support; I need none other', he was heard to mutter to himself.

In a statement to the press he said:

> 'Man proposes, God disposes' has come true often enough in my life, as it probably has in the case of many others. When I left Calcutta on Sunday last, I knew nothing about the sad state of things in Delhi. But since my arrival in the capital city, I have been listening the whole day long to the tale of woe that is

Delhi today. I have seen several Muslim friends who recited to me their pathetic story. I have heard enough to warn me that I must not leave Delhi for the Punjab until it has once again become its former peaceful self.

I must do my little bit to calm the heated atmosphere. I must apply the old formula. 'Do or Die' to the capital of India.

From 10th September, Gandhiji set out to make a tour of the riot-affected parts of the city and the various Muslim and Hindu refugee camps.

He asked all the refugees to live truly, fearlessly and at the same time without malice or hatred towards anybody. Let them not throw away the golden apple of dearly won-freedom by hasty and thoughtless action in the moment of anger.

In the course of his post-prayer address at evening, Gandhiji remarked that he was anxious to go to Pakistan and test for himself the reality of Jinnah's professions. The Hindus of Pakistan were their brothers, he had declared. They would look after them as such and feed them before feeding even themselves. Were these brave words meant only to tickle the ears of the world? But he could not go there owing to the disturbances in Delhi. It would not do for either Dominion to plead helplessness and say that, it was all the work of the ruffians. Each Dominion must bear full responsibility for the acts of those who lived in it.

The bulk of the police force of Delhi was Muslim. A number of them, with their uniform and arms, had deserted. The loyalty of the rest was doubtful. Sardar Patel had to wire for reliable Gurkha police from West Bengal. A contingent of 250 constables with some sub-inspectors of police was sent by Chief Minister of the Central Provinces in response to an urgent message from Sardar.

The Sardar was at the end of his nerves. During one of his visits to the city one day he found that firing had been going on incessantly from a building occupied by the Muslims for the last twenty-four hours. "Why has this pocket not been cleared?" he asked a high military officer accompanying him. The latter replied that this was not possible with the force at their disposal unless they blew up building. "Then why did not you do it?" The Sardar snapped.

In the prayer meeting that evening Gandhiji appealed to the people to forget the past and not to brood over their sufferings but extend the right hand of fellowship to one another, determine to live in peace. The Muslims should be proud to belong to the Indian Union and show due respect to the tricolour.

On 13th September Gandhiji visited the Muslim refugee camp at Purana Quila. The refugees were in a very ugly mood. As soon as Gandhiji's car entered the gate, crowds of them rushed out of their tents and surrounded it. Anti-Gandhi slogans were shouted.

Referring to his experience at Purana Quila and other refugee camps, Gandhiji said that he had met their angry faces and he had seen the same beam with love. It would be madness to make the present estrangement into a permanent enmity. Transfer of population was a fatal snare. It would only mean greater misery. The solution lay in both the communities living in their original homes in peace and friendship. "I plead for a frank and bold acknowledgement by the respective Governments of the misdeeds of their majority communities. It is the bounden duty of each Dominion to guarantee full protection to its minorities."

In a written message to his evening prayer gathering on 14th September Gandhi said:

> These thoughts have haunted me throughout these last twenty hours. My silence has been a blessing. It has made me inquire within. Have the citizens of Delhi gone mad? Have they no humanity left in them? Have love of the country and its freedom no appeal

> for them? I must be pardoned for putting the first blame on the Hindus and the Sikhs. Could they not be men enough to stem the tide of hatred? I would urge the Muslims of Delhi to shed all fear, trust God and discover all the arms in their possession which the Hindus and Sikhs fear they have. Either the minority rely upon God and His creature man to do the right thing or rely upon their firearms to defend themselves against those whom, they feel, they must not trust.

During the two weeks that Gandhiji had been in the capital the initial fury of the outbreak had been brought under control.

3

The Greatest Fast

Some Maulanas of Delhi came to see Gandhiji on 11th January. One of them said: "How long do you expect the Muslims to put up with these pin-pricks? If the Congress cannot guarantee their protection, let them plainly say so. The Muslims will then go away and be at least spared the daily insults and possible physical violence. For ourselves we cannot even go to Pakistan for as nationalist Muslims we have been opposed to its formation. On the other hand, the Hindus will not allow us to live in the capital. So we cannot stay, in the Indian Union either. Why not arrange a passage for us and send us to England, if you cannot guarantee our safety and self-respect here?"

"You call yourselves nationalist Muslims and you speak like this?" Gandhiji answered reproachfully. But the steely barb had entered into his heart. It was the last straw. "We are steadily losing grip on Delhi", he remarked to a friend. "If Delhi goes, India goes and with that the last hope of world peace".

On 12th January in the afternoon, Gandhiji was as usual sitting out on the lawn of Birla House. As it was Monday, his day of weekly silence, he was writing out his prayer address. As Sushila Nayar looked through sheet after sheet that she was to translate and read out to the prayer congregation in the evening, she was dumb-founded. She came running to

Pyarelal with the news—Gandhiji has decided to launch on a fast unto death unless the madness in Delhi ceased.

The written address containing the decision was read out at the evening prayer meeting. The fast would begin on the next day after the mid-day meal. There would be no time limit. During the fast he would take only water with or without salt and the juice of sour limes. The fast would be terminated only when and if he was satisfied that there was a reunion of hearts of all communities brought about without outside pressure but from an awakened sense of duty.

The statement ran:

> One fasts for health's sake under laws governing health or fast as a penance for a wrong done and felt as such. In these fasts, the fasting one need not believe in Ahimsa. There is, however, a fast which a votary of non-violence sometimes feels impelled to undertake by way of protest against some wrong done by society and this he does when he as a votary of Ahimsa has no other remedy left. Such an occasion has come my way.
>
> When, I returned to Delhi from Calcutta on 9th September, 1947, gay Delhi looked a city of the dead. At once I saw that I had to be in Delhi and 'do or die'. There is apparent calm brought about by prompt military and police action. But there is storm within the breast. It may burst forth any day. This I count as no fulfillment of the vow to 'do' which alone can keep me from death the incomparable friend....
>
> I never like to feel resourceless, a Satyagrahi never should.... My impotence has been gnawing at me of late. It will go immediately the fast is undertaken. I have been brooding over it for the last three days. The final conclusion has flashed upon me and it makes me happy. No man, if he is pure, has any thing more precious to give than his life. I hope and pray that I have that purity in me to justify the step.

The statement continued:

> I flatter myself with the belief that loss of her soul by India will mean the loss of the hope of aching storm-tossed and hungry world. Let no friend or foe, if there be one, be angry with me. There are friends who do not believe in the method of the fast for the reclamation of the human mind. They will bear with me and extend to me the same liberty of action that they claim for themselves. With God as my supreme and sole counselor, I felt that I must take the decision without any adviser. If I have made a mistake and discover it, I shall have no hesitation in proclaiming it from the house top and retracting my faulty step. There is little chance of my making such a discovery.... I plead for all absence of argument and inevitable endorsement of the step. If the whole of India responds or at least Delhi does, the fast might soon be ended.
>
> But whether it ends soon or late or never, let there be no softness in dealing with what may be termed as a crisis.... A pure fast, like duty, is its own reward. I do not embark upon it for the sake of the result, it may bring. I do so because, I must. Hence, I urge everybody dispassionately to examine the purpose and let me die. If I must, in peace which I hope is ensured. Death for me would be glorious deliverance rather than that I should be a helpless witness of the destruction of India. Hinduism, Sikhism and Islam. That destruction is certain if Pakistan ensures no equality of status and security of life and property for all professing the various faiths of the world and if India copies her. Only then Islam dies in the two India's, not in the world. But Hinduism and Sikhism have no world outside India.

The statement concluded with an appeal:

> Those who differ from me will be honored by me for their resistance however implacable. Let my fast quicken conscience, not deaden it. Just contemplate the rot that has set in beloved India and your will rejoice to think that there is an humble son of hers who is strong enough and possibly pure enough to take the happy step. If he is neither, he is a burden on earth. The sooner he disappears and clears the Indian atmosphere of the burden better for him and all concerned.

In reply to a question as to why he should have decided to launch on a fast at that juncture when nothing extraordinary happened, he answered that death by inches was far worse than sudden death. It would have been foolish for me to wait till the last Muslim has been turned out of Delhi by subtle undemocratic methods.

Devdas, Gandhiji's youngest son, made an attempt to dissuade his father from the grave decision. In a note sent to Gandhiji he said: "My chief concern and my argument against your fast is that you have surrendered to impatience, whereas your mission by its very nature calls for infinite patience. You do not seem to have realized what a tremendous success your patient labor has achieved. It has saved thousands of lives and may still save many more.... By your death you will not be able to accomplish what you can by living. I would, therefore beseech you to pay heed to my entreaty and give up your decision to fast".

In reply Gandhiji wrote to Devdas: "...It was only when in terms of human effort, I had exhausted all resources and realized my utter helplessness that I laid my head on God's lap. That is the inner meaning and significance of my fast. You would do well to read and ponder over Gajendra Moksha—the greatest of devotional poems as I have called it. Then alone, perhaps, you will be able to appreciate the step I have taken,...Strive while you live is beautiful saying, but there is a hiatus in it. Striving has to be in the spirit of detachment. Now perhaps you will understand why I cannot comply with your request. God sent this fast. He alone will end it, if and when He wills. In the meantime it behoves you, me and everybody to have faith that it is equally well whether he preserves my life or ends it, and to act accordingly. I can therefore, only pray that He may lend strength to my spirit lest the desire to live may tempt me into premature termination of my fast".

The fast commenced at 11.55 a.m. on the 13th January with the singing of *Vaishnava Jana*, and 'When I Survey the Wondrous Cross' sung by Sushila Nayar followed by Ramadhun.

Describing his fast as my greatest fast, in a letter to Mirabehan dated 16th January, Gandhiji wrote. "Whether it will ultimately prove so or not is neither your concern nor mine. Our concern is the act itself and not the result of action."

A Muslim friend entreated Gandhiji to give up the fast for the sake of Muslims. "You are only our hope and support," he pleaded. "The Muslims are not innocent. Have not the Hindus and Sikhs too suffered beyond words. I know that," Gandhiji replied, "That is the very reason why I am fasting. I shall become a broken reed and be lost to both Hindus and Muslims, like salt that hath lost its savor, if in this hour of test, I fall to live up to my creed and their expectations."

Sheikh Abdullah, the Prime Minister of Kashmir with Bakshi Ghulam Mohammad, the Deputy Prime Minister, had come down to Delhi. They too, requested Gandhiji to end his fast for the sake of Kashmir. Kashmir needs you now more than ever. They said that they would not return to Kashmir till he complied with their request. Gandhiji told them that his fast was intended to cover Kashmir also.

Maulana Abul Kalam Azad intervened and said: "Even if we were to dash our heads against a stone wall, his resolve once taken will not be given up. To argue further with him is only to prolong his agony. The only thing for us is to begin thinking what we can do to fulfill his conditions which alone will induce him to give up his fast." And so they all set about to tackle the problem constructively.

A deputation of Hindu and Sikh refugees came next. Gandhiji told them that it was in their hands to terminate his fast. "There should be a thorough cleansing of hearts. You should be able to give assurance that even if the whole of India goes up in a blaze, Delhi will be safe. If you do not pay heed to my words now, you will all weep and wring your hands in sorrow afterwards."

At the evening prayer meeting Gandhiji declared that he would break his fast only when conditions in Delhi permitted the withdrawal of the military and police without any danger to peace. The police might remain but only to cope with anti-social elements, not for enforcing communal peace.

Some people had complained that the Mahatma had sympathy for the Muslims only and had undertaken the fast for their sake. Gandhiji answered that in a sense they were right. All his life he had stood, as every one should stand, for minorities or those in need. Pakistan had resulted in depriving the Muslims of the Union of their pride and self-confidence. It hurt him to think that this should be so. It weakened the foundations of a State to have any class of people lose self-confidence. His fast was against the Muslims too, in the sense that it should enable them to stand up to their Hindu and Sikh brethren. In terms of his fast, therefore, Muslim friends had to exert themselves no less than the Hindus and Sikhs. He wanted a thorough all-round cleansing of hearts as a result of his fast. They should dethrone Satan from their hearts and reinstate God. He could not break the fast for less. It did not matter how long it took for real peace to be established. No-one should say or do anything to hire him into giving up his fast permanently. The object should not be to save his life but to save India and her honor.

When the Delhi Maulanas came to see him, Gandhiji greeted them with, "Are you now satisfied?" Then, turning to the one who had said to him that he should get the Union Government to send them to England, he remarked: "I had no answer to give you then, I can now face you. Shall I ask the Government to arrange a passage for you to England? I shall say to them: Here are the unfaithful Muslims who want to desert India. Give them the facility they want."

The Maulana said he felt sorry if his words had hurt him. Gandhiji retorted: "That would be like the Englishman who kicks you and at the same time goes on saying, I beg your pardon!" Becoming serious he proceeded: "Do you not feel ashamed of asking to be sent to England? And then you said that slavery under British rule was better than independence under the Union of India. How dare you, who claim to be patriots and nationalist, utter such words? You have to cleanse your hearts and learn to be cent per cent truthful. Otherwise India will not tolerate you for long and even I shall not be able to help you."

At the evening prayer meeting, he spoke about the cold-blooded attack on the refugee train at Gujrat, and the programme against the Hindus and Sikhs at Karachi. A new note of confidence and strength rang through his speech. How long can the Union put up with such things? How long can I bank upon the patience of the Hindus and Sikhs in spite of my fast? Pakistan has to put a stop to this state of affairs. They must pledge themselves that they will not rest till the Hindus and Sikhs can return and live in safety in Pakistan.

He drew a glowing picture of what would happen if there was a wave of self-purification all over India. "Pakistan will become pak (pure).... Past things will have forgotten, past distinction will have been buried, the least and the smallest in Pakistan will command the same respect and same protection of life and property can never die. Then and not till then shall I repeat that I ever called it a sin, as I am afraid I must hold today. It is I want to live to see the Pakistan not on paper, not in the orations of Pakistani orators, but in the daily life of every Pakistani Muslim. Then the inhabitants of the Union will forget that there ever was any enmity between them and if I am not mistaken, the Union will proudly copy Pakistan and if I am alive I shall ask her to excel Pakistan in well-doing. The fast is a bid for nothing less." He admitted that to India's shame there were some in the Union who readily copied Pakistan's bad manners.

He further said: "I have not the slightest desire that the fast should be ended as quickly as possible. It matters little if the ecstatic wishes of a fool like me are never realized and the fast never broken. I am content to wait as long as it may be necessary, but it will hurt me to think that people have acted merely in order to save my life. I claim that God has inspired this fast.... No human agency has ever been known to thwart nor will it ever thwart Divine Will."

A stream of messages of sympathy and support poured in from Muslim leaders and Muslim organizations all over India and even from abroad. There were telegrams from the Nizam of Hyderabad and Nawabs of Rampur and Bhopal. The President of the Bombay provincial Muslim League, in a statement, characterized Gandhiji's fast as 'a challenge to Hindus, Muslims and Sikhs...to save.... Hinduism, Islam and Sikhism.' He appealed all to contribute their mite in restoring peace for the sake of our country and religion.

Of particular significance was an injunction by a Muslim divine from Barelly to his followers. "There is no greater friend of Musalmans than you, whether to Pakistan or Hindustan. My heart bleeds with yours at recent Karachi and Gujrat atrocities, the massacre of innocent men, women and children, forcible conversion and the abduction of women. These are crimes against Allah for which there is no pardon. Let the Pakistan Government know that. Much less can an Islamic State be founded upon such heinous crimes against Allah's creation. I order my followers in Pakistan and appeal to the Pakistan Muslims and Government to put an end to these shameful, un-Islamic misdeeds and express unqualified repentance. My order to my followers and to the Muslims of Hindustan is that they must remain loyal to you and to the Union Government to the last...condemn the misdeeds of their co-religionists in Pakistan in unambiguous and emphatic terms to create public abhorrence against such action. It is high time that Musalmans should realize that their sincere loyalty to the Union and their leaders confidence in themselves are the only safeguards that can protect them. The secret desire to look to Pakistan for guidance and help will be their doom. Pray break your fast and save Hindustan and Pakistan from ruin, disaster and death."

Ever since the Great Calcutta Killing of August 1946, Gandhiji had been telling Muslims that if they continued to sit on fence instead of courageously denouncing the excesses of their co-religionists and failed to align themselves with the victims of the same even at the risk of their lives, or if they harbored secret sympathy with the perpetrators of those excesses, it would bring down upon them the wrath of those with whom—Pakistan or no Pakistan—the bulk of them must live.... At the commencement of his fast he had told a group of Maulanas, who came to request him to reverse his decision, that if happenings like the recent massacre of the Hindu and Sikh refugees on the train at Gujrat continued unchecked, not to speak of himself, even ten Gandhis would not be able to save the Indian Muslims. He reinforced that appeal with a few straight words of his own. "It is impossible to save the lives of the Muslims in the Union," he warned, "if the Muslim majority in Pakistan do not behave as decent men and women."

Addressing a rally of some ten thousand people, Hindus and Sikhs, Pandit Nehru said: "The loss of Mahatma Gandhiji's life would mean the loss of India's soul, because he is the embodiment of India's spiritual power.... Like a prophet, he has realized that communal, fighting if not checked immediately, would bring about the end of freedom".

All India Radio started to broadcast hourly bulletins on Gandhiji's condition. Everywhere in India save Gandhiji's life committees sprang up. There was not a mosque in India that did not pray for him at Friday Namaz. The untouchables of Bombay sent a moving cable telling Gandhiji, "Your life belongs to us".

Hindus and Sikhs and Muslims formed Peace Brigades marching through the capital begging Gandhiji to give up his fast. Most moving of all, 200 women and children, widowed and orphaned by the slaughter of the Punjab, paraded to Birla House declaring that they were going to renounce their miserable refugees' relations to join a fast of sympathy with Gandhiji.

'I am in no hurry,' Gandhiji told the worried crowd at his prayer meeting in a voice that, even magnified by loudspeakers, was barely a whisper. "I do not wish things half done. I would cease to have any interest in life, if peace were not established all around us over the whole of India, the whole of Pakistan," he said.

Nehru came with a delegation of leaders to assure Gandhiji that there had been radical change in Delhi's atmosphere. Gandhiji told him, "Do not worry, I will not pop off suddenly. Whatever you do, should ring true. I want solid work."

On the fifth day Sushila Nayar's bulletin said: "it is our duty to tell the people to take immediate steps to produce the requisite conditions for ending Bapu's fast without further delay."

Gandhiji dictated to Pyarelal seven conditions for ending his fast.

Mountbatten and his wife Edwina came to see Gandhiji 'Ah.' Gandhi exclaimed: "It takes a fast on my part to bring the mountain to Mohamed".

On the afternoon of Saturday 17, Gandhiji told his prayer gathering: "It is not within anybody's power to save my life or end it. It is only in God's power." He also told the audience, "Today, he saw no reasoning for ending his fast."

Nehru moved to the microphone and said, "I saw the freedom of India as a vision. I had charted the future of Asia in my heart. It was Gandhi, an odd-looking man with no art of dressing and no polish in his way of speech who had given him that vision." He further said, "There is something great and vital in the soul of our country which can produce a Gandhi. No sacrifice was too great to save him, because only he can lead us to the true goal and not the false dawn of our hopes".

Pyarelal came and told Gandhiji that Peace Committee has pledged to restore peace, harmony and have all the leaders signed the pledge? Pyarelal hesitantly told that except Hindu Mahasabha and R.S.S., all others have signed. Gandhiji shook his head and said: "No, I will not break my fast until the stoniest heart melted."

Rajendra Prasad came and told Gandhiji: "Seven point conditions now bore all the signatures he had requested. It was their unanimous deeply felt wish that he break his fast." One by one, the men around Gandhiji's bed confirmed Prasad's words with their own. Gandhiji indicated that he wanted to speak.

In a low voice he said: "Nothing could be more foolish than to think that India must be for Hindus and Pakistan for Muslims alone. It is difficult to reform the whole of India and Pakistan, but if we set our hearts on something, it must become a reality."

"If, after listening to all this, you will want me to give up my fast, I shall do so. But if India does not change for the better, what you say is a mere, farce, there will be nothing left for me but to die".

Gandhiji then agreed to break his fast, which was done with the ceremony of prayers. The text from the Koran, Zendavesta, and Gita were recited, followed by the mantra:

Lead me from untruth to truth,
From darkness to light
From death to immortality.

A Christian hymn was sung followed by Ramdhun. The glass of orange juice was handed by Maulana Abul Kalam Azad and Gandhiji broke the last of his historic fast on the 18th January 1948 at 12.45 noon.

Gandhiji addressed his prayer meeting in the evening in which he said: "I can never forget all my life the kindness shown to me by all of you. Do not differentiate between Delhi and other places. Let peace return to all India and Pakistan as well. If we remember that all life is one, there is no reason why we should treat one another as enemies. Let every Hindu study the Koran, let Muslims ponder over the meaning of the Gita, and the Sikhs the Granth Sahib."

He further said, "As we respect our own religion so must we respect other people's. What is just and right is just and right. Whether it be inspired in Sanskrit, Urdu, Persian or any other language. May God bestow sanity on us and the whole world. May He make us wiser and draw us closer to Him so that India and the whole world may be happy."

Everybody agreed. Hindus and Muslims alike: men great and men humble that it was Gandhiji, who by his presence in Calcutta saved Bengal from civil strife and it was again he who finally extinguished communal flames in Delhi. As Jesus calmed the storm on the sea of Galiles, Gandhiji calmed and ended the storm of hate and madness, for which he had to undergo all agony.

Jawaharlal Nehru said: "How many realize what it meant to India to have the presence of Gandhiji during these months? We all know of his magnificence services to India to freedom during the past half century and more. But no service could have been greater than what he has performed during the last four months. When in a dissolving world, he has been like a rock of purpose and a light house of truth, and his firm low voice has risen above the clamors of the multitude pointing out the path of rightful endeavors."

4

Lost Desire to Live 125 Years

At the All India Congress Committee meeting in Bombay on 8th August 1942, that is, on the eve of Quit India Movement, Mahatma Gandhi declared.

I want to live full span of my life and according to me, the full span of life is 125. By that time, India will not only be free but the whole world will be free.

Thereafter in *Harijanbandhu* dated 11th February 1946, under the caption living upto 125, he wrote "I have not talked about wishing to live the age of 125 years without thought. It has a deep significance. The basis for my wish is the third Mantra from *Ishopanishad*, which literally rendered, means that a man should desire to live for 100 years, while serving with detachment. One commentary says that 100 really means 125.... It is service in a spirit of detachment, which means complete independence of the fruit of action.... I have not the slightest doubt that without attaining that state of detachment; it is impossible to live to be 125 years old."

On 2nd October 1947, when the congratulations were pouring in, he went to the extent of saying: "...Where do congratulations come in. There is nothing but anguish in my heart. There was a time, whatever I said, masses followed. Today, mine is a lone voice.... I have been told that I have no place in the new order.... I have no desire to live."

Gandhiji refused to release for publication any of the birthday messages—telegrams or letters—which had come from all parts of the world.

Lord Ismay, Chief of the Viceroy's staff, prayed that Gandhiji might long be spared to lead us along the path of peace.

Lord Mountbatten wrote: "You hold a unique position in the eyes of the world as a whole. Never has your gospel of non-violence been more needed than it is now. Long may you be spared to spread it."

A message from the High Commissioner of Pakistan in India, Zahid Hussain, ran: "Today the people of India—in which I include Pakistan—are suffering untold miseries and privations resulting from hatreds and conflicts. All eyes are turned on Mahatma Gandhi in the unparalleled crisis which has overtaken the country. India is in many ways a key to the future of the human race and we all hope and pray that inspired by the ideals of Mahatma Gandhi, she will play part truly and well."

"How much has happened since we celebrated it last year?" wrote Lord Pethic—Lawrence, who on the eve of the transfer of power had retired from the post of Secretary of State for India. "Neither you nor I are of course fully satisfied with the final outcome. But international progress, like true love, never runs quite smoothly and what has been won is infinitely greater than what has been lost. I devoutly hope that the recent tragic events though they remain a scar on the fair face of India will not continue as a running score."

In a separate note, Lady Pethic-Lawrence who was in her 80th year, recalling that day (2nd October) happened to be their own wedding day, too, wrote: "What an influence you have had upon the history of the world—yes, and will continue to have for years to come! You told me last year that you intended to celebrate your centenary! I hope with all my heart that it may be so and that every year may be more full of confident faith than the preceding one."

Sarojini Naidu was due to retire shortly from the Governorship of the United Provinces. In a note pulsating with affection and vivacity, which even her chronic invalidism could not damp, she wrote: "My days of being a she-Lat (Lady Governor) are coming to the end by the end of October and I shall be a free bird out of the cage again. It is only rarely that I yield to my constant temptation to intrude on your thought or time, if only as lightly and briefly as a butterfly. Today I yield both to the desire and temptation and send you one little word of greeting. I am now partially convinced that I am really rather a sweet old lady!"

Sir Stafford Cripps, watching from a distance the tribulation through which Gandhiji had been passing since partition and burdened perhaps with the consciousness that the British power could not be altogether absolved from a share in the tragedies that had overtaken India, wrote:

> I have purposely refrained from writing to you in the most anxious and perilous times through which you and your country—or your two countries!—have been passing.... All your friends in this country—and they are many-admire greatly the determined way in which you have set out to conquer the evil by good. It has been a great inspiration for all of us, who have the good of India at heart. We have been made so sad at all that has happened and we are only too conscious of the part that the past history has played in the present discontents. I pray that you may be given the strength to preserve and that by your example the evil spirit of communal faction will die down so that India and Pakistan may resume their progress towards what I shall hope one day be the goal of unity.

In his after prayer speech on 4th October, Gandhi said: "The Hindus and Muslims today seemed to vie with each other in cruelty. Even women, children and aged were not spared. He had worked hard for the independence of India and prayed to God to let him live up to 125 years so that he could see the establishment of *Ramarajya*—the Kingdom of Heaven on Earth, in India. But today there was no such prospect before them. The people had taken the law into their own hands. Was he to be helpless witness of the tragedy? He prayed to God to give him the strength to make them see their error and mend it, or else remove him. Time was when their love for him made them follow implicitly. Their affection had not perhaps died down, but his appeal to their reason and hearts seemed to have lost its force. Was it that they had use for him only while they were slaves and had none in an independent India? Did independence mean goodbye to civilization and humanity? He could not give them any other message now than the one he had proclaimed from house-tops all these years."

A French friend expostulated with Gandhiji. He had already achieved so much and after all, if God was responsible for every happening, He will bring out good out of evil. Therefore Gandhiji should not feel depressed. "In my opinion this (Gandhiji's despondency) is the final attempt for the forces of evil to foil the divine plan of India's contribution to the solution of the world's distress by way of non-violence. You are today the only instrument in the world to further the divine purpose."

But Gandhiji could not, as he put it, allow himself to be deceived by kind words. No-one could live on his past, he replied. He could wish to live only if he felt that that he could render service to the people, i.e. make the people see the error of their ways. He had put himself entirely in God's hands. If God wished to take further work from him, He would. But, if he was not able to render more service, it would be best that God took him away.

A couple of days later, in an article in *Harijan*, he wrote that it was wrong to describe his state of mind as one of depression. Only he was not vain enough to think that the divine purpose could be fulfilled only through him.

It is likely as not that a fitter instrument will be used to carry it out and that I was good enough to represent a weak nation, not a strong one. May it not be that a man purer, more courageous, more far-seeing is wanted for the final purpose? This is all speculation. No-one has the capacity to judge God. We are drops in that limitless ocean of mercy. Without doubt the ideal thing would be neither to wish to live, nor to wish to die. Mine must be a state of complete resignation to the Divine Will.

But having had the 'impertinence' openly to declare his wish to live 125 years, he felt, he in changed circumstances, must have the 'humility' openly to shed that, wish. "I (therefore) invoke the aid of the all-embracing Power to take me away from this vale of tears rather than make me a helpless witness of the butchery by man become savage.... Yet I cry. Not my will but Thine alone shall prevail. If He wants me, He will keep me here on this earth yet a while".

"There is a place of peace beneath all the turmoil where spirits can meet," an English woman wrote to Gandhiji. She was not disturbed, she said by the pronouncements that seemed to upset so many people. He does not want to live, they say—he is losing faith, he advocates war etc. But I seem to catch an echo in your words of that cry of the soul that came from Christ Himself. If it be Thy will let this cup pass from me. God knows what agony you must be passing through. I sense that much will be demanded of you and that the respite you sometimes crave will not come yet. If it does, I shall not grieve that you have gone. I selfishly want you to stay here with us in this terrible world, and help us. But already you have spent a life-time of ceaseless toil and labor of love, trying to turn men's thoughts into the Way of Truth and non-violence. I have little doubt that India has touched bottom only to rise to immense heights. It is the work that you have done all these years that will show her how to rise.

She quoted from a letter she had received from the late Mahadev Desai in 1941, when England was fighting single-handed with the Germans: "You have a terrible heavy cross to bear—not only that of bombing, homelessness and starvation, but of making ignorant people understand that we in India are friends, not enemies. It is a frightfully difficult task, I know, but you who know and understand Bapuji so well can cope with." To her Gandhiji replied: "The cross of which Mahadev wrote to you years ago whilst he was yet alive was nothing compared to the Cross that presses one today."

An American friend wrote to Gandhiji that it was but natural that he should feel 'a degree of disillusionment' because of the sad happenings that had of late overtaken India. But that disillusionment should be measured and certainly not turn into discouragement. Never does the seed turn directly into a beautiful fragrant flower without first going through certain phases of growth and development. And if at some state its development—or growth—it falters, the presence of the gardener is more than ever required.

Replying to it Gandhiji wrote in *Harijan*: "What they say may prove true and the senseless blood-bath through which India is still passing may be nothing unusual as history goes. What India is passing through must be regarded as unusual, if we grant that such liberty as India has gained was a tribute to non-violence." But as he had repeatedly said, he went on to say, non-violence of India's struggle was only in name. "In reality it was passive resistance of the weak. The truth of the statement we see demonstrated by the happenings in India."

And again: "Hope for the future I have never lost and never will.... What has, however, clearly happened in my case is the discovery that in all probability there is a vital defect in my technique of the working of non-violence. There was no real appreciation of non-violence in the thirty years struggle against British Raj. Therefore the peace that the masses maintained during that struggle of a generation with exemplary patience had not come from within. The pent up fury found an outlet when British Raj was gone. It naturally vented itself in communal violence which was never fully absent and which was kept under suppression by the British bayonet. Failure of my technique of non-violence causes no loss of faith in non-violence itself. On the contrary that faith is, if possible strengthened by the discovery of a possible flaw in the technique."

Miss Schlesin, his devoted secretary of South African days, unable to realize her dream to rejoining him in India, had been following from distant South Africa the development of his thought and activities. She wrote: "Far from losing your desire to live until you are 125 increasing knowledge of the world's lovelessness and consequent misery should cause you rather to determine to live longer still. In view of your decision to live at least so long, your remark about fatalism is not understood—what of *immanent* Divine, the indwelling god? You said in a letter to me some time ago that every one ought to wish to attain the age of 125—you cannot go back on that."

To her Gandhiji replied: "Usually your letters are models of accurate thinking. This one before me is not. You talk of my decision to live 125 years, I never could make any such foolish and impossible decision. It is beyond the capacity of human being. He can only wish again. I never expressed an unconditional wish. My wish was conditional upon continuous act of service of mankind. If that act fails me, as it seems to be failing in India, I must not only cease to wish to attain that age, but should wish the contrary as I am doing now."

5
Second Crucifixion

On 28th January 1948, Rajkumari Amrit Kaur asked Gandhiji, "Were there noises in your prayer meeting today?" "No," said Gandhiji. "But does the question mean that you are worrying about me? If I am to die by the bullet of a mad man, I must do so smiling. There must be no anger within me. God must be in my heart and on my lips. And you promise me one thing. Should such a thing happen, you are not to shed one tear."

The whole of 29th January was so full of activity that at the end of the day Gandhiji was utterly fired. His head was reeling. 'And yet I must finish this,' he remarked pointing to the draft constitution for the Congress, which he had undertaken to prepare for the Working Committee. He rose at quarter past nine to retire to bed. He was feeling very much disturbed and he recited to Manu a Urdu couplet, meaning:

> The spring of the garden of the world lasts for a few days; Have a look at its show for a few days.

On the fateful Friday the 30th January, Gandhiji woke up as usual at the Brahamamuharta i.e. 3.00 a.m. He was still coughing and he had not yet recovered from the effects of his fast. His mind dwelling on the woman—who was absent from the prayer—he said, "I do not like these signs. I hope God does not keep me here very long to witness these things."

Gandhiji used to take plam-jaggery lozenges with powdered cloves to ally his cough. The clove powder had run out, Manu, therefore, instead of joining him sat down to prepare some. "I shall join you later," she said to him, "otherwise there will be nothing at hand at night when it is needed." Gandhiji did not like anyone missing his duty in the immediate present to anticipate and provide for the uncertain future. "Who knows, what is going to happen before nightfall or even whether I shall be alive?" he said to Manu and then added: "If at night I am still alive you can easily prepare then some."

Manu asked Gandhiji what prayer she should chant for him. He asked her to chant an old Gujrati hymn which reflected his own restlessness and brooding anxiety:

> Whether weary or un-weary, O Man, do not rest,
> Do not cease your single-handed struggle.
> Go on, and do not rest.
> You will follow confused and tangled pathways,
> And you will save only a few sorrowful lives.
> O Man, do not lose faith, do not rest.
> Your own life will be exhausting and crippling,
> And there will be growing dangers on the journey.
> O Man, bear all these burdens, do not rest.
> Leap over your troubles though they are high as mountains,
> And though there are only dry and barren fields beyond.
> O Man, till those fields, do not rest.
> The world will be dark and you shall shed light on it,
> And you shall dispel all the darkness around.
> O Man, though life deserts you, do not rest.
> O Man, take no rest for thyself,
> O Man, give rest unto others.

Passing through Pyarelal's room, he handed him the draft of a new constitution for the Congress—his *Last Will and Testament* to the Nation—which he had partly prepared on the previous night, and he asked Pyarelal to go through it carefully. "Fill in any gaps that you find in my thinking. I prepared it under heavy strain." He was still at his meal when Pyarelal took to him the draft constitution of the Congress. He carefully went through the additions and alterations, point by point, and removed an errors calculation that had crept in with regard to the number of the Panchayat leaders.

After his midday nap, Gandhiji saw some Maulanas from Delhi, who gave their consent to his going to Sevagram. He told them that he would be absent for a short while only, unless God willed it otherwise and something unforeseen happened.

He told to Bishan: "Bring me my important letters. I must reply to them today, for tomorrow I may never be."

Sardar Patel with his daughter came to see Gandhiji at 4 p.m. Gandhiji had a talk with him for over one hour, while spinning. He told the Sardar, that one of the two-either the Sardar or Pandit Nehru—should withdraw from the Cabinet, he had since come to the firm conclusion that the presence there of both of them was indispensable. Any breach in their ranks at that stage would be disastrous. He further said, he would make that the topic of his post prayer-speech in the evening. Pandit Nehru would be seeing him after the prayer, he would discuss the question with him too. If necessary he would postpone his going to Sevagram and not leave Delhi till he had finally laid the spectre of disunity between the two.

Manu entered the room to say that two Congress leaders from Kathiawad had arrived and would like to spend a few minutes with him. Gandhiji replied: "Tell them that they can talk to me during my walk after the prayer meeting. If I am still alive."

At 5 p.m. Gandhiji took out his watch and told the Sardar that it is time for his prayer. He left his room at 5.10 p.m.

to wend his way to the prayer congregation on the adjoining lawn. Manu and Abha were by his side. He leaned on them as he walked. As he passed through the cordoned path through the prayer congregation, he took his hands off the shoulders of those two girls to acknowledge the greetings of the people. All of a sudden, a Hindu named Nathuram Godse, elbowed his way through the crowd. Manu thinking that he was coming forward to touch Gandhiji's feet, remonstrated and tried to stop the intruder by holding his hand. He violently jerked her off, and bending before Gandhiji with his palms folded, as if in the act of making obeisance, fired point-blank three shots in quick succession from a seven-chambered automatic pistol. All the bullets hit Gandhiji on and below the chest on the right side. Two bullets passed right through, the third bullet remained embedded in the lung. At the first shot, the foot that was in motion faltered. The hands which had been raised in *namaskar* slowly came down. He still stood on his legs; then the second and third shot rang out and he collapsed. He uttered *He Rama*. The face turned ashen grey. Crimson spot appeared on the white clothes. The body was carried inside and laid on the matress, where he used to sit and work. Death was instantaneous (*Mahatma,* Vol. vii: D.G. Tendulkar, p. 288).

Gandhiji died as he wanted to die, facing his enemy smiling and saying the name of God.

The assassin, Nathuram Godse, was grappled by the Birla House gardener. Raghu Mali, and was with the help of others overpowered after a short scuffle.

First to arrive at Birla House was Sardar Patel. He sat by the side of Bapu with his wan, haggard face like granite. Next came Jawaharlal Nehru and burying his face in Gandhiji's clothes sobbed like a child. Sardar Patel consoled him, affectionately patting him on the back. Devadas, the Mahatma's youngest son, followed and tenderly taking his father's hand into his, burst into tears. Then came others: Maulana Azad, Jairamdas Daulatram, Rajkumari Amrit Kaur,

Acharya Kripalani and K.M. Munshi. Lord Mountbatten had returned from Madras by air that very day, leaving behind Lady Mountbatten to complete her engagements in the city. When he arrived at Birla House, the rush outside had become so great that he could get in only with difficulty.

A suggestion was made for embalming Gandhiji's body and keeping it in state at least for a period. Knowing how uncompromising Gandhiji's opposition was to a fetish being made of the physical body after death, Pyarelal felt it to be his sacred duty to intervene. "But that would be contrary to Bapu's wishes," he whispered into Dr. Jivraj Mehta's ear. "Then you must tell him." Dr. Mehta said to Pyarelal and pushed him forward. "Your Excellency," Pyarelal said addressing Mountbatten, "it is my duty to tell you that Gandhiji strongly disapproved of the practice of embalming and he gave me specific standing instructions that his body should be cremated wherever his death occurred." Dr. Jivraj Mehta and Jairamdas Daulatram supported Pyarelal.

"If he had died in the normal course, full of years and honors," Mountbatten said, "that would have been alright. But considering the special circumstances, do not think...? He paused, making a gesture of interrogation with his outstretched hand."

Pyarelal answered: "Gandhiji told me, even in my death I shall chide you if you fail in your duty in this respect."

"His wishes shall be respected," said Mountbatten. And so the idea of embalming was given up.

At night Pandit Nehru's voice was heard on the All-India Radio: "Friends.... The light has gone out of our lives and there is darkness everywhere and I do not quite know what to tell you and how to say it. Our beloved leader Bapu as we called him, the Father of our Nation, is no more. Perhaps I am wrong to say that. Nevertheless we will not see him again as we have seen him these many years. We will not run to him for advice and seek solace from him, and that is a terrible blow not to me only but to millions and millions in this country. And it is difficult to soften the blow by any advice that I or anyone else can give you.

"The light has gone out, I said, and yet I was wrong. For the light that shone in this country was not ordinary light. The light that has illumined this country for these many years will illumine this country for many more years, and a thousand years later that light will still be seen in this country, and the world will see it and it will give solace to innumerable hearts. For that light represented the living truth reminding us of the right path, drawing us from error, taking this ancient country to freedom.

"All this has happened. There is so much more to do. There was so much more for him to do. We could never think that he was unnecessary or that he has done his task. But now, particularly, when we are faced with so many difficulties, his not being with us is a blow most terrible to bear."

In the small hours of the night, the body was bathed and anointed with sandalwood paste and then laid down in the middle of the room covered with flowers. The members of the Diplomatic Corps came and paid silent homage to the departed one, laying their wreaths at his feet.

Once more the dead body was taken upstairs and placed upon the balcony to enable the milling crowd below to have final *darshan*.

Following the strict dictates of Hindu custom. Manu and Abha smeared fresh cow-dung over the marble floor of Birla House to prepare it to receive Gandhi's corpse. When Gandhi's sons and secretaries had given him a final bath, his body was rapped in a winding-sheet of homespun cotton and set on the floor on a wooden plank. A Brahmin priest anointed his chest with sandalwood paste and saffron. Manu pressed a vermilion dot upon his forehead. Then she and Abha lovingly wrote 'Hey Rama' in laurel leaves at his head and 'Om' in rose petals at his feet.

Then before giving the body of their beloved Bapu back to a waiting world, they performed a final gesture. They all knew how Gandhi hated the Hindu custom of garlanding the defunct with wreaths of flowers. And so Devadas knotted around his father's neck a loop of homespun cotton yarn cut from the threads he had turned that afternoon with the last revolution of his cherished spinning-wheel (*Freedom at Midnight: Dominique Lapierre & Larry Collins*, p. 561).

At 11.30 a.m. the bier was taken out of Birla House and placed in a weapon-carrier hung with flags and festooned with flowers.

The Defence Ministry had taken over charge of the arrangements of the funeral. The undertaking was so colossal that it was deemed to be altogether beyond the capacity of any voluntary organization to tackle it. With the whole city in a state of turmoil, the possibility of a commotion being touched off which might envelop the whole country in a chain reaction of violence, was frightening. The army had overnight converted the chassis of a weapon-carrier to serve as a bier. On a raised platform in the middle of it rested the dead body, covered with a while, green and saffron national flag and half buried under the mass of wreaths, garlands and flowers. On the right side of the bier sat Ramadas, Gandhiji's third son, on the left Sardar Patel and Devadas Gandhi in front. Nehru, Kripalani, Rajendra Prasad took up their places beside the bier. Other members of Gandhiji's family and leaders took their turns on the vehicle by the side of the bier or walked behind the cortege chanting Ramadhun.

A party of 200 men from the army, the navy and the air force drew the carriage by four stout ropes. The engine was kept shut throughout. 4000 soldiers, 1000 airmen, 1000 policemen and 100 sailors walked in front and behind the bier. Lancers on horse-back flying white pennants—the Governor-General's bodyguard—led the way. All through the journey soldiers, policemen and armored cars helped in controlling the crowd.

The cortege extremely slowly inch by inch in a mournful silence broken only by an occasional muffled roar of *Mahatma Gandhi ki Jai.* After an hour the War Memorial arch was reached. People had got on to the base of King George Fifth's statue by wading through the surrounding pool. They hung on to the pillars supporting the stone canopy, were seen perched on the top of the 150 feet high War Memorial, on the lamp and telephone posts, and among the branches of the trees on both sides of the route, to have a better view of the cortege as it passed below. The entire Central Vista was a vast, ant-heap of humanity, looking from a distance almost motionless. Three planes of the air force swooped repeatedly down showering flowers as the procession moved down the Hardinge Avenue and approached Delhi Gate.

At 4.20 p.m. the procession reached the Rajghat cremation ground by the side of the Yamuna. Bier was taken down from the weapon carrier and laid on a raised platform that had been built near the funeral pyre for the performance of the final rites before the cremation. At 4.30 the body was placed on the funeral pyre. Fifteen mounds of sandal wood, four mounds of ghee, two mounds of incense, one mound of coconuts and fifteen seers of camphor had been collected for the cremation. Flower garlands and wreaths were placed at the feet of the dead body, the Chinese Ambassador, doyen of the Diplomatic Corps in the capital leading. The Indian national flag that covered the bier was then removed. Devadas Gandhi piled logs of sandalwood on the body of his father which was sprinkled with the holy Ganges water. The funeral pyre was lit by his elder brother Ramadas in the absence of Harilal to the chanting of Vedic hymns.

It was now 4.45 p.m. As tongues of fire began slowly to crawl up among the logs, mass round the pyre rose to pay a last homage to the Father of the Nation by observing one minute's silence. A thunderous shout went up from the vast gathering, *Mahatma Gandhi Amar Ho Gaye*—Mahatma Gandhi has become immortal. In that final rite, as the flames, consumed the earthly remains of the Mahatma, was symbolized the fulfillment of the Vedic prayer:

> Lead me from the Unreal to the Real
> From Darkness to Light
> From Death to immortality

The sweet fragrance of the incense filled the whole atmosphere. Soon the blaze became too fierce for those seated in the front rows to remain there. By 6 p.m. the Mahatma's remains were completely reduced to ashes.

All night while the funeral pyre cooled, the mourners filed silently past the smoking remains of what had once been a great man. Lost among them, unrecognized and unremarked, was the man who should have lit those flames, a derelict ravaged by alcohol and tuberculosis. Gandhiji's eldest son Harilal.

At first light Nehru laid a little bouquet of roses on the still smoldering ashes. "Bapuji," he said "here are flowers. Today at least I can offer them to your bones and ashes. Where will I offer them tomorrow and to whom?"

Jawaharlal Nehru in his speech in Parliament on 2nd February said: "Great men and eminent, men have monuments in bronze and marble set up for them, but this man of divine fire managed in his life time to become enmeshed in millions and millions hearts so that all of us have become somewhat of the stuff that he was made of, though to an infinitely lesser degree. He spread out over India, not only in palaces or in select places or in assemblies, but even in hamlet and hut of the lowly and of those who suffer. He lived in the hearts of millions and he will live for unmemorable ages."

In an article published in 'Harijan' on 2nd February 1948. Nehru wrote: "Even in his death there was a magnificence and complete artistry. It was from every point of view a fitting climax to the man and to the life he had lived. He died in the fullness of his powers and as he would no doubt have liked to die, at the moment of prayer. He died a martyr to the cause of unity to which he had always been devoted and for which he had worked unceasingly. He lived and died at the top of his strength and powers, leaving a picture in our minds and in the minds of the age that we lived in the age that can never fade away."

The ten-day interval between the collection of ashes and their immersion was a period of prayerful heart-searching for all. "After I am gone, no single person will be able completely to represent me." Gandhiji used to say. "But a little bit of me will live in many of you. If each puts the cause first and himself last. The vacuum will to a large extent be filled."

There were some who wanted the bones to be housed in a great mausoleum where they would be honored through all the generations to come. Once more Pyarelal, stepped forward, insisting that Gandhiji had specifically objected to any memorials and wanted no special honors paid to him. It was decided that the *asthis*, should be cast into the waters at Allahabad, at the Triveni Sangam.

Thirteen days after the cremation the bones were gathered up and placed in a copper urn. A special train carried the flower-decked urn to Allahabad, stopping at the wayside stations to let the people have their last darshan. At Allahabad the urn was mounted on an enormous truck for the short journey from the railway station to the river, and then it was taken down and placed on a small amphibious landing craft, with Nehru, Patel, Maulana Azad, Ramadas and Devadas, Manu and Abha to watch over it until the bones were emptied into the river. Dakotas flew overhead, dropping roses and soon the landing craft turned toward the shore.

The ashes of the Mahatma were off on the last pilgrimage of a devout Hindu, their long voyage to the sea and the mystic instant when the eternal mother, the Ganges, would deposit them in the eternity of the ocean, and Gandhiji's soul, outsourcing the shadows of the night, would become one with the *Mahat*, the Supreme, the God of his celestial *Gita*.

Gandhiji was always ready to die. He renewed his readiness to die at the level of intention everyday and demonstrated in action a hundred time. Perhaps, most notably on the occasion of his assassination. There were more than one such occasions. The first in South Africa, when he agreed to the compromise in registration of Indians as suggested by General Smutts. One, Pathan by name Mir Alam, who had been Gandhiji's client and had often gone to him for advice swore that he would kill the first person to register. As Gandhiji was about to enter the registration office as first person, Mir Alam hit him on the head, knocking him unconscious.

On another occasion, Mahadev Desai received a letter from the Private Secretary to Lord Linlithgo, saying that the German wireless had broadcast the news that the British agents are planning to the assassination of Gandhiji and asked him: "Would Gandhiji like to have unobtrusive police placed around him. His Excellency would be very glad to arrange it." Mahadev Desai under instructions from Gandhiji replied: "Gandhiji wants no such thing as having lived under the threat of assassination for a generation, he had come to learn by experience that not a blade of grass moves except by His will and no assassin can curtail anybody's life or a friend protect him."

Yet on another occasion, Gandhiji said: "Ever since I took the pledge of service. I have dedicated my head to humanity. It is the easiest thing in the world to chop off my head. It does not take the slightest preparation or organization. And outside help I have never sought. In fact, it is futile, to think protecting me for I know that God Almighty is the only protector. When my time is up, no one, not even the most renowned can stand between Him and me." He further said: "To die by the hand of a brother, rather than by disease or in such other way, cannot be a matter of sorrow for me. And even, if in such a case I am free from the thoughts of anger or hatred against my assailant. I know that I will redound to my eternal welfare and even the assailant will later on realize my perfect innocence."

He continued: "But if some one were to shoot me in the belief that he was getting rid of a rascal, he will kill not the real Gandhi, but the one that appeared to him a rascal. I might be killed but Gandhism cannot be killed. If non-violence can be killed, Gandhism can be killed." In 1919 he said: "My desire is to close this life searching for truth, acting for truth and thinking for truth and truth alone."

Once Gandhiji sent the following message to commemorate the martyrdom of a co-worker:

> My ahimsa will be perfect, if I could die peacefully with axe blows on my head. I have always been dreaming of such a death and I wish to treasure this dream. How noble that death will be a dagger attack at me from one side, an axe blow from another direction and kicks and abuses from all sides and if in the midst of all these I could ask others to act and behave likewise and finally I could die with cheer on my face and smile on my lips then and then alone my ahimsa will be perfect and true. I am hankering after such an opportunity.

On another occasion Gandhiji said: "If some one were to tell me in order to avoid death to retire to Himalayas, I shall not do so for I know that death is inevitable, no matter what precautions man deludes himself with. God knows what work to take out from me. He will not permit me to live for a moment longer than He needs me for His work."

What a glorious end, what an enviable death at the age of 79 in full possession and vigorous exercise of all God-given faculties, at the zenith of his glory-venerated by 400 millions of his countrymen as the Prophet who led them by the world at large as the greatest revolutionary who fought and won freedom's battle with the unique weapons of truth and non-violence.

None in mankind's long history had been blessed a unique reunion with the Maker.

In death, as in life, Gandhiji set a model for his fellowmen to emulate. He died with the name of God on his lips with his hand folded in humility and reverence.

In sum:

> Gandhiji was frail in physique but mighty in spirit.
>
> Every inch of land that, he trod, was sanctified.
>
> His mere presence spread solace and was a benediction.
>
> He saved the lives of millions; for his own safety he cared not.
>
> Blessed is, the nation that gave birth to so precious a Gem of humanity.
>
> Blessed is the generation that had the privilege to live during the lifetime of this Martyr Saint.
>
> Blessed are the multitudes who had the good fortune to witness this apostle of ahimsa move about in flesh and blood.
>
> Blessed are followers and fellow-workers who had the golden opportunity to serve the Motherland under the inspiration and guidance of this God-man.
>
> He was a "Tyagaatma". Embodiment of silent, selflessness that found joy and fulfillment in sacrifice.
>
> He was a "Satyaatma" uncompromising votary of truth.
>
> He was a "Snehaatma" effluent symbol of brotherhood of man.
>
> He was a "Dharmmatma" peerless personification of Righteousness.

Above all, he was a 'Mahatma' sublime synonym for Comprehension and Compassion to all alike, from the highest to the lowliest and the lost, nay to the smallest of God's creation.

As he lived, so he died—in the service of the, Lord and, for the welfare of his fellowmen—the crowning glory, the Grand Finale of the Greatest Life of the 20th Century.

Over 2500 and odd years ago was born Lord Buddha. But Buddhism took roots and spread only after two or three hundred years after the nirvana of Buddha.

Likewise, Jesus of Nazareth was born two centuries before. But Christianity started flourishing only after hundreds of years after Lord Jesus was crucified.

In his sermon on Mahatma on 12th March 1922 in Chicago, USA, Rev. John Holmes said: "...If we would classify Gandhi with any of the supreme figures of human, it must be with such august prophets as Confucius and Laotse, Buddha, Zoroaster, and Mohammed and most truly of all the Nazarene."

Holmes further said: "In all reverence and with due regard to historic fact, match this man with Jesus Christ. If the lives of these two were written side by side as Plutarch wrote the lives of the great heroes of Greece and Rome, it would be amazing to see to what extent they are identical.

"As Gandhi moves from place to place great multitudes of men and women follow him as similar multitude followed Jesus in Palestine.... In humility, in sacrifice, in ardent love of men, he is one of those perfect characters which come along once in a thousand or perhaps only in two thousand years.... A society which cannot suffer a Jesus or a Gandhi to be at large is a society which is not fit to live. By this token it is already doomed to die.... If I believed in the 'second coming' as I do not, I should dare to assert that Gandhi was Jesus come back to Earth. But, if 'second coming' has no historical validity, it has at least poetical significance and in this sense, can we not speak of Gandhi as indeed the—Jesus."

It is worth recollecting what Dr. Martin Luther King said of Gandhiji.

"Gandhiji was probably the first person in history to lift the love of ethic of Jesus above mere interaction between individual to a powerful and effective social force on a large scale. Love, for Gandhi, was a patent instrument for social and collective transformation. It was in this Gandhian emphasis on love and non-violence that I discovered the method for social reform that I had been seeking for so many months. The intellectual and moral satisfaction that I failed to gain from the utilitarianism of Bentham and Mill, the revolutionary method of Marx and Lenin, the social-contract theory of Hobbes, the 'Back to Nature' optimism of Rousseau, and the superman philosophy of Nitzsche, I found in the non-violent resistance philosophy of Gandhi. I came to feel that this was the only morally and practically sound method open to oppressed people in their struggle for freedom."

Shri S. Ramakishnan, the Executive Secretary and Director General of Bharatiya Vidya Bhavan described Gandhiji as follows in the book, *Mahatma Gandhi: External Pilgrim of Peace and Love*, collated by me (pp. 46-52).

No messiah in recorded history, save him, commanded such spontaneous, free and willing allegiance of millions and millions in his own life time. Popular recognition and acceptance came to the most of world-teachers only after they had left the scene of their labors.

He transformed an unarmed, forlorn, politically-subjugated and by and large, dumb and illiterate mass of humanity into a fearless, non-violent, politically-awakened, resurgent militia for constructive national service and ready to 'Do or Die' for the freedom and progress of the motherland.

With soul-force, he successfully shook the foundations of the mightiest ever-Empire on earth, and led us from bondage to freedom.

He lived and labored in, the faith and experienced the truth of the refrain of the famous hymn—of the poet-saints of

India like Surdas, Tulsidas, Kabirdas, Ramadas, Purandaradas, Bilvarunangal, Chaitanya, Thyagaraja, Vidyapat, Narsi and others.

His life was an epic-saga of saintliness, selflessness, suffering and sacrifice.

He was the luminous symbol of 'nonpareil' of the incessant, throbbing, living flow of India's ageless religion and culture.

He was the confluence 'Sangam' of all that is best and noblest in Indian culture from the Vedic age to the Modern Indian renaissance.

Like the rishis of the old, he was an exemplar of austere living and high thinking, virtuous in his life and work.

Like Maryada Purushottam Shri Ramchandra, he was tenaciously resolute in honoring the plighted word. He yielded not pressure or persuasion to take the path of expediency and to swerve from the path of righteousness. Neither did he resort to semantic jugglery or subterfuge to circumvent and unpleasant, of his duty-Swadharma.

Like Poorna Purushottam Sri Krishna, to him Right was Might: thought not followed by action and deception, and preaching without practice was treachery.

Like the Venerable Bhisma Pitamaha, he was inflexible in his resolve and terribly earnest in everything he said and did.

Like Ajatshatru Dharmaputra, he looked at his own shortcomings through a magnifying glass and applied the highest standards; while to the shortcomings of others, he showed understanding and applied the common standards.

Like Gautama Buddha, he was a man of boundless love, mercy and compassion but an uncompromising, opponent of the hypocrisy and humbug.

Like Verdhaman Mahavira, he was one of the noblest apostles of non-violence.

Like Adi Shankaracharya, he was one of the greatest redeemers of Hinduism.

Like Ramakrishna Paramhansa, he was a man of prayer, immense humility and catholicity.

Like Swami Vivekananda, he was cyclonic patriot-saint, a unique revolutionary and incomparable social-reformer *sans peur et san reproche*. His heart bled for the poor and the downtrodden.

Truth was his God and God's name—Ramanama—was his staff of life.

He was a 'Nishkama Karmayogi,' he labored dispassionately without attachment to results.

He was the embodiment for 'abhaya'—fearlessness, not merely physical courage, but the total absence of fear from the mind, born of unshakable faith in the Almighty and complete surrender unto His Will.

True to the definition of scripture—*Manasyekam, Vachasyekam, Karmaneykam, Mahatmanam*—he was real Mahatma. There was a complete accord between his thought, word and deed.

He had all the attributes of an Abhijata as expounded by Lord Krishna in *Bhagvad Gita*.

He was devoted Hindu, who lived up to the highest ideals of the Sanatan Dharma as strictly observed the Mahavrat-ahimsa, satya, asteya, brahmacharya, aprigraha.

He saw divinity in every soul. To him, all fellow-beings were part of his own flesh and blood and the world one family—Vasudhaiva Kutumbakam.

Such a man, who was considered the Father of the Nation, hailed next to Buddha and Jesus, equated with the Saints of India has been assassinated, Why?

6
World Mourned for Mahatma Gandhi

Gandhiji's assassination caused dismay and pain throughout India. It was as though the three bullets that entered his body had pierced the flesh of tens of millions. The nation was baffled, stunned and hurt by the sudden news that this man of peace, who loved his enemies and would not have killed an insect, had been shot dead by his own countrymen and co-religionist.

Never in modern history has any man been mourned more deeply and more widely.

The Indian authorities received 3441 messages of sympathy, all unsolicited from foreign countries. For Gandhi was a moral man, and a civilization not richly endowed with morality felt still further impoverished when the assassin's bullets ended his life. "Mahatma Gandhi was the spokesman for the conscience of all mankind," said General George C. Marshall, United States Secretary of State.

Pope Pius, the Dalai Lama, the Archbishop of Canterbury, the Chief Rabbi of London, the King of England, President Truman, Chiang Kai-shek, the President of France, indeed the political heads of all important countries and most minor ones publicly expressed their grief at Gandhi's passing.

Leon Blum, the French Socialist, put on paper what millions felt. 'I never saw Gandhi,' Blum wrote. "I do and know his language. I never set foot in his country and yet I feel the same sorrow as if I had lost someone near and dear. The whole world has been plunged into mourning by the death of this extraordinary man."

'Gandhi had demonstrated,' Professor Albert Einstein asserted, "that a powerful human following can be assembled not only through the cunning game of the usual political maneuvers and trickeries but through the cogent example of a morally superior conduct of life. In our time of utter moral decadence he was the only statesman to stand for a higher human relationship in the political sphere. Generations to come will scare believe that such a one as this ever in flesh and blood will be upon this earth."

The Security Council of the United Nations paused for its members to pay tribute to the dead man. Philip Noel-Baker, the British representative, praised Gandhi as 'the friend of the poorest and the lowliest and the lost.' Gandhi's greatest achievement,' he predicted, 'are still to come'. Other members of the Security Council extolled Gandhi's spiritual qualities and lauded his devotion to peace and non-violence. Mr. Andrei Gromyko, of the Soviet Union, called Gandhi 'one of the outstanding political leaders of India' whose name 'will always be linked with the struggle of the Indian people for their national liberation which has lasted over such a long period.' Soviet Ukraine delegate Tarasenko also stressed Gandhi's politics.

The U.N. lowered its flag to half-mast.
Humanity lowered its flag.

The world-wide response to Gandhi's death was in itself an important fact; it revealed a widespread mood and need. "There is still some hope for the world which reacted as reverently as it did to the death of Gandhi," Albert Deutsch declared in the New York newspaper *PH*. "The shock and sorrow that followed the New Delhi tragedy shows we still respect sainthood even when we cannot fully understand it."

Gandhi "made humility and simple truth more powerful than empires", U.S. Senator Arthur H. Vandenberg said. Justice Felix Frankfurter called it "a cruel blow against the forces of good in the world".

General Douglas MacArthur, supreme Allied military commander in Japan, said: "In the evolution of civilization, if it is to survive, all men cannot fail eventually to adopt Gandhi's belief that the process of mass application of force to resolve contentious issues is fundamentally not only wrong but contains within itself the germs of self-destruction." Lord (Admiral) Mountbatten, last British Viceroy in India, expressed the hope that Gandhi's life might 'inspire our troubled world to save itself by following his noble example.' The spectacle of the general and the admiral pinning their faith on the verdict of Sir Hartley Shawcross, British Attorney General, that Gandhi was 'the most remarkable man of the century.'

A California girl of thirteen wrote in a letter: "I was really terribly sad to hear about Gandhi's death. I never knew I was that interested in him, but I found myself quite unhappy about the great man's death."

'I know no other man of any time or indeed in recent history,' wrote Sir Stafford Cripps, "who so forcefully and convincingly demonstrated the power of spirit over material things. This is what the people sensed when they mourned. All around them, material things had power over spirit. The sudden flash of his death revealed a vast darkness. No one who survived him had tried so hard—and with so much success—to live a life of truth, kindness, self-effacement, humility, service and non-violence throughout a long, difficult struggle against mighty adversaries. He fought passionately and unremittingly against British rule of his country and against the evil in his own countrymen. But he kept his hands clean in the midst of battle. He fought without malice or falsehood or hate" (*The Life of Mahatma Gandhi: Louis Fischer,* pp. 9-13).

C. Rajagopalachari—the conscience keeper of Mahatma Gandhi says: "No one could die a more glorious death than Mahatma Gandhi. He was going to the seat of his prayer to speak to his Rama. He did not die in a bed calling for hot water, doctors or nurses. He did not die after mumbling incoherent words in the sick bed. He died standing, not even sitting down. Rama was too eager, even before he could reach the seat of his prayer."

Mrs. Mary Bethune, American Negro Leader said: "Gandhi cannot die, his spirit is free to stir men's souls in every corner of the earth. As we, mothers of the earth, stand in awesome fear of the roar of Jet planes, the crash of atom bombs, and the unknown horrors of germ warfare, we must turn our eyes in hope to East where the sun of Mahatma blazes."

Pearl S. Buck said: "India will leave and become great in the world, only as her people use the force of non-violence, which the life of Gandhi exemplified for them. He did what he told others to do. When people saw that this was true, they believed in him. Gandhi has done his part. It now remains for the people of India to take upon themselves his world leadership for non-violence."

Pearl Buck further said: "Indeed it is the only way in which can fulfill the promise of her greatness of violence the world is sick. By hatreds and quarrels we are surfeited and poisoned. The hearts of the peoples turn away from the noise of militarists and warmongers. We long for the peace makers. No war brings peace, for violence only brings more violence." Buck described Gandhi's assassination as another crucifixion.

In 1932, Gandhiji was designated as the sole representative of the Indian National Congress to participate in the Second Round Table Conference in London convened by Prime Minister Ramsay McDonald of British Labour Party. Politely declining the British Government's special arrangements, Gandhiji opted to stay in East London where the underprivileged resided. Fenner Brockway his host, would see him for discussion—political and philosophical—at 8 a.m. everyday while Gandhi would be spinning. One day he asked Gandhiji, Jesus Christ has decreed, "Love Thy enemies". What is your comment? Gandhiji smiled but did not answer. After fifteen minutes of further discussion covering other topics, Brockway reverted to the subject. Reluctantly the Mahatma said: "Fenner, I have no enemies. Therefore the question of loving or hating does not arise". Deeply moved Fenner Brockway said: "This proves you are greater than Jesus".

On the martyrdom of Gandhiji, the same Mr. Fenner Brockway wrote: "The world has lost its greatest figure.... Perhaps history, too, has its greatest figure...the whole world will catch his spirit and shall move towards the peace which Mahatma Gandhi loved."

J.B. Kripalani, in his book, *Gandhi: His Life and Thought*, on pages 301 and 302 writes: "The voice that had guided and warned us for more than thirty years was thus silenced. The light that had led us on to our goal was extinguished. But can an assassin's bullet or dagger silence the voice or extinguish the light of the chosen of the Gods who have a mission to perform? They never die. They live as long as their message has meaning and relevance for humanity. It would be hard to deny that Gandhiji's message of peace and goodwill is needed by humanity in this nuclear age more than ever before. His message may not be heard in the land of his birth. But was his message only for his people? It was for the whole of humanity. Those who had ears to hear heard its echo in America with the martyrdom of Martin Luther King Jr., a true follower of Gandhiji. Wherever people yearn for life and light, Gandhiji's voice will prevail.

"The most cruel part of this tragedy is not only the death of Gandhiji. It is that he fell by the blow struck by one who considered himself a Hindu, against one who had ordered his life in the spirit of *Upanishads and Gita*. The assassin has betrayed the whole history of Hinduism, which never raised its hand against a spiritual teacher for the views he held, however heterodox they were considered by a section of his people. The Hindus have not only tolerated but even welcomed differences in belief, honestly held and propagated. It was for such misguided people, who injure their religion while seeking to protect it through violence and murder, that it was said: God, forgive them, for they know not what they do."

Death comes to all, but death by assassination seems to be an end reserved for the very greatest and least deserving. The history recalls many instances. Jesus Christ, Julious Caesar, Abraham Lincoln, John F. Kennedy, Martin Luther King to mention a few.

Caesar dead is more powerful than Caesar alive. The crucifixion of Jesus Christ resulted in a great religion coming to birth, which moulded the thoughts and minds of billions of people. The death of Gandhiji brought into existence a philosophy which is not only the basis of State craft in our country, but influenced people all over the world.

7

Mindset behind Gandhi's Assassination

Years ago Romain Rolland declared that he regarded Gandhi as a 'Christ who only lacked the Cross.' Rolland further said, "Gandhi has renewed for all the people of the West the message of their Christ, forgotten or betrayed. He has inscribed his name among the sages and saints of humanity and the radiance of his figure has penetrated all the regions of the earth."

When Gandhiji died the Government of India received more than 3441 messages expressing condolences from foreign countries alone. They included tributes from King George, President Harry S. Truman, Prime Minister Clemet Atlee, Mrs. Eleanor Roosevelt, and scores of others. The Ministry of Information declared: "Perhaps no man in recorded history received such spontaneous tributes of universal praise, reverence and love as did Mahatma Gandhi at his death." Never before had such a flood of love and sympathy been poured out on the death of Gandhiji. People of every land poured out their affection.

But there were two persons from India, who did not recognize the greatness of Gandhiji, during his life time. They also did not show magnanimity of their heart and mind after

Gandhiji's assassination. They were Mohammed Ali Jinnah and Dr. B.R. Ambedkar.

In his letter of 8th February 1948 to Sharda alias Laxmi Kabir, who later became his wife, Ambedkar Wrote:

> My own view is that great men are of great service to their country, but they are also at certain times a great hindrance to the progress of their country. There is one incidence in Roman history which comes to my mind on this occasion. When Caesar was done to death and the matter was reported to Cicero. Cicero said to messenger. "Tell the Romans your hour of liberty has come." While one regrets the assassination of Mr. Gandhi, one cannot help finding in his heart the echo of the sentiments expressed by Cicero on the assassination of Caesar. Mr. Gandhi had become a positive danger to this country. He had choked all the thoughts. He was holding together the Congress, which is a combination of all bad and self-seeking elements in society who agreed on no social or moral principle governing the life of society except the one praising and flattering Mr. Gandhi. Such a body is unfit to govern a country. As the Bible says that some times good cometh out of evil, so also I think that good will come out of the death of Mr. Gandhi. It will release people from bondage to superman, it will make them think themselves and it will compel them to stand on their own merits.

Justice Chandrashekhar Dharmadhikari says:

> In Pune, a well established and prominent religious leader has recently said that the bones of Godse have been kept in safe custody. Even the entire family of Godse was honoured publicly in Pune. It is also being asserted that Godse had done a religious act by assassinating Gandhi. Gandhi's murder is being called Gandhi *vadha*. The term *vadha* is used for the

> murder of a miscreant like Kansa and Ravana. A man who dares to engage in such heroic and good cause deserves all praise from the society. Both Lord Rama and Lord Krishna were praised for Ravana vadha and Kansa vadha respectively. Godse committed Gandhi vadha not his murder according to such people. Hence he deserves all praise! Could it be any thing more atrocious than this? Did Gandhi become a miscreant by instilling a deep sense of unity among our people. Have these people gone out of their heads? The fact of the matter is that Godse was not just an individual. He represents a mindset—a way of thinking. Such people believe that, if they physically eliminate a person, they might succeed in killing his thoughts, his world view. They did not have the capacity to engage in an ideological warfare with such eminent people. Hence, they decide to murder them in the hope that their way of thinking would end along with their physical dissolution. That is why all great people of the world have suffered at the hands of assassins. But history has proved otherwise. The thought processes of such great people gather greater momentum after their physical elimination.

"But these people hardly want to learn from history. Godse and his ilk thought that by murdering Gandhi, they could very well eliminate his thought processes. This tendency among a small section of diehard conservatives is even taking deeper roots. It is they who challenge the idea of Gandhi being the father of the nation. Through that challenge they want to destroy the very nationhood of India. Such tendency is fast growing in our country."

Justice Chandrashekhar Dharmadhikari, in his article in Contemplating Gandhi writes:

> There is a new anti-Gandhi wave in Maharashtra. It has even reached a stage of xenophobia. Whether it is a drama on Nathuram Godse (I am Nathuram Godse

> speaking) or films on Babasaheb Ambedkar, Bhagat Singh or Savarkar; in all of them, Gandhi is being depicted either as a villain or as a comical character. The reason behind such attempts is that all these leaders are being projected as men of destiny. On the other hand, there is a deliberate attempt to undermine Gandhi and his role in history. Even the scene of Gandhi's assassination is being presented in such a way that it should evoke thunderous clapping from the audience. The act of assassination is eulogized. It is clear that this is the only way they could extol their heroes. Thus there is a concerted attempt at character assassination of Gandhi. This is a part of a well designed conspiracy.

It is this mindset which has prompted them to use the word *Gandhivadh*. The Sanskrit word *vadh* is usually used while depicting the murder of demons or bad people. Such a murder is taken to be a religious act. My strong objection is to the use of *vadh* in respect of Gandhi's assassination. Some of these anti-Gandhi people have gone to the extent of showing me a dictionary to say that the three words, *khoon* (bloodshed), *hatya* (murder), *vadh* (killing of demons) are synonyms. They do not know that synonymous words given in a dictionary do not necessarily convey the same meaning. We have to look at their popular connotations. If these three words are taken as synonymous then can one say that the word *khoon* could be used in case of Ravan *vadh* by Lord Rama or in the case of Afazal Khan's killing by Chhatrapati Shivaji Maharaj. They will never accept it. When people are unable to contest someone's ideas they resort to murder. They think that in such a way both the concerned person and his ideas could be finished forever. That is why Bernard Shaw said: "that the ultimate form of censorship is assassination." Nathuram Godse truly represented that mindset and these people engaged in anti-Gandhi drama or films are also of the same genre. It was in this contest Khalil Gibran said that ultimately all the great people like Socrates, Christ, Abraham Lincoln, Joan of Arc are martyred. If Gibran could have lived for a few years more, I am sure that he would have included the names of Mahatma Gandhi and Martin Luther King Jr. in the list.

Malice towards Gandhi was not new to Maharashtra. Tendulkar, Pyarelal and other authors have written that at least five murder attempts had been made on Gandhi's life in Maharashtra. A bomb was thrown on Mahatma Gandhi in Pune in 1934. In July 1944 when Gandhi was undergoing treatment at Panchgani, a group of 18-20 people went there including Nathuram Godse. He started shouting at Gandhi and the latter called him inside. Then Godse took out a knife from his jacket and attempted an attack on Gandhi. Again when Gandhi was coming from Mumbai to Pune an attempt was made to blow up the train. But this attempt failed due to the driver's swift and ingenious action. Another attempt was made on Gandhi's life when he was at his *ashram* in Sevagram. Ultimately Godse succeeded in assassinating him on January 30, 1948. The supporters of Godse wanted to finally bury the Mahatma forever. Why all these happened only in Maharashtra? That is the question before me. Now it is happening in Gandhi's Gujarat, it seems that all these are a part of a larger conspiracy.

Some time back Sudarshan, the chief of RSS came out with an astounding statement that the Quit India Movement of 1942 with Gandhi's clarion call of 'Do or Die' was meaningless and without having any direction. That is why the RSS did not participate in it. In January 2001, in BJP Today, a publication of BJP, had also raised the question whether freedom movement was really needed or not. According to the editor of the paper, had India patiently waited for independence then would it have not got independence as an undivided country? There was no need for struggle for independence and India could have got independence in the due course of time. In that case, there would not have been problems like Kashmir, Pakistan and Bangladesh and the suffering which the people went through during freedom struggle could have been easily avoided.

The paper has attached a list of 45 countries that got their independence in the similar way. However, the paper did concede that Gandhi was not in a hurry to get independence as he was insisting on undivided India. The Muslim League and its leader Jinnah were against it. Nehru was too much in a hurry to get independence and it is he who became its greatest beneficiary. If we could have simply waited without launching the freedom movement, we could have easily got a united and independent India. It is in such a political approach that the seeds of malice towards Gandhi are to be found. It also displays the lack of knowledge about India's struggle for independence.

On the one hand, they have been maintaining that no one has got independence without struggle. Then how the same people are saying we could have got independence as a matter of gift from the British. It is nothing short of a great insult for all those who fought for independence from 1857 onward including Savarkar, Subhash Chandra Bose and other revolutionaries. Even if we leave out the question of how Indian history is being distorted by these people, the real question is how long we would go on tolerating such mindless insult and humiliation to our revolutionaries and freedom fighters? This is an insidious and elitist attempt to mislead and misguide today's youth. There are still some people around, who think that the British rule was better than the present one. They could have stayed in their high positions and continued to live at the exploitation of the poor and the dispossessed. The youth should understand their mindset.

Here it is very relevant to refer to the speech delivered by Mahatma Gandhi on 8 August 1942, on the eve of launching of the Quit India Movement. Gandhi gave a new mantra to the people of India in his speech.

Here is a mantra, a short one that I give you. You may imprint it on your hearts and let every breath of yours give expression to it. The mantra is: "Do or Die." We shall either free India or die in the attempt; we shall not live to see perpetuation of our slavery. Every true Congressman or (Congress) woman will join the struggle with an inflexible determination not to remain alive to see the country in bondage and slavery. Let that be your pledge.

Take a pledge with God and your own conscience as witness that you will no longer rest till freedom is achieved and will be prepared to lay down your lives in the attempt to achieve it. He who loses his life will gain it; he who will seek to save it shall lose it.

The direction for freedom fighters and the common people given by Gandhi in his speech is crystal clear. But those inspired by Godse's mindset and ludicrous idea of Gandhi *vadh* save their lives by their non-participation in the struggle. In the words of Gandhi they lost their lives in their attempt to save it by running away from the struggle. What one could say about these spineless and lifeless people? They could not understand Gandhi and would never understand it.

It is such a Godse mentality which is responsible for everyday killing of some of the best ideas given by Gandhi like truth, non-violence, compassion, and purity of life and thought. Referring to the spread of such mindset one of the Hindi poets has written:

> Oh Gandhi! It is good you died at the right time otherwise you would be dying everyday. We commemorate Gandhi martyrdom day on 30 January every year. What could be more painful that Gandhi's assassination is also being staged by people of this mindset? We have to think seriously even after his martyrdom anti-Gandhi wave is not subsiding and a campaign based on untruth and lie is being continuously launched. We may recall that out of the

five attempts on Gandhi's life, Godse was involved in three of them.

Gandhi wrote a letter to the Viceroy of India, regarding Bhagat Singh's case and pleaded with him for reducing punishment given to him. He also wrote a piece in *Young India* praising him for his bravery, sacrifice and his commitment to the country. Earlier Gandhi had expressed similar feelings in respect of Vir Savarkar. He not only wrote regarding Savarkar but also went to Ratnagiri to see him. Both of them differed on the issue of the pathway to independence of India, but Gandhi never lagged behind in pleading for Savarkar's release. Subsequently, Savarkar changed his direction. He was an accused in Gandhi's assassination case but was exonerated in the absence of credible evidence. However, he was not free from the blemish in the anti-Gandhi campaign. He was primarily brought into the anti-Gandhi campaign by his own followers. One would simply wonder whether his followers were his well-wisher or his enemies.

This is what exactly is happening in respect of Dr. B.R. Ambedkar. Both respected each other. It was on Gandhi's initiative that Ambedkar was made the Minister of Law, Government of India and subsequently as the Chairman of the Drafting Committee of the Constituent Assembly. Ambedkar stood for the liberation of the downtrodden section of our society. He was working for their liberation from social, economic and all other kinds of slavery. He was supportive of Gandhi's service to the *Harijan's* but his followers were trying to bring them to their own level and make him fight against Gandhi. In this kind of struggle who ultimately wins become immaterial. But the land on which these contests take place is ruined in the process. That is the real tragedy.

Why should we sow the seeds of hatred in the minds of the younger generations who have not seen the leaders of previous generations like Gandhi, Savarkar, Bhagat Singh and Ambedkar. One has to consider what kind of self-interest such people have? In the name of great people, no one should seek to promote his own interest, otherwise the coming generation will never forgive us.

Those who stress on religiosity in India are the real blood brothers of Jinnah. In their view differences based on religion and region are artificial but they don't accept the unity of all human beings. That is why a man like Gandhi who propounded man oriented Indianness appears as an enemy in their eyes. In fact, their entire politics is based on hatred, revenge and religious fanaticism. That is the primary reason for their anti-Gandhi bias.

The man in the street looks at Gandhi and his ideas with hope and expectation. It is the only shelter they can look forward to. These anti-Gandhi elements want to deprive the common man from their last source of support and succour. They have the implicit if not explicit support of some political parties. We cannot forget that there were such elements who indulged in sinful acts of distributing sweets after his assassination. Even today there are people in Maharashtra who are willing to celebrate Godse's day of demise. The only thing left to be done is to get a postal stamp in the name of Godse to put him on the high pedestal or to seek Bharat Ratna for him posthumously? I will not be surprised if these elements try to make such ridiculous attempts to glorify Godse and his cohorts.

For religious fanatics, religion is matter of exploitation, revenge and investment. Such people are determined to teach a lesson to the people of other religions. This is a symbol of their murderous inclination and butcher's mentality and that is why they take out their deep feeling of revenge by putting the scene of Gandhi's assassination through drama, cinema and publication of different kinds of literature. All these are done by groups of fanatic Hindus. Their *Hindutva* is based on their animus against Muslims and Gandhi. Murder and violence are found to be their mainstay. They take devilish pleasure in watching anti-Gandhi scenes. They clap, shout and even tear out Gandhi's photos and destroy his statues. Perhaps they want to put a statue of Godse in place of Gandhi.

They could never understand Gandhi or his philosophy nor do they have the desire to do so. They have blinkers on their eyes. Regimentation and indoctrination have been their faith. The whole scenario has been beautifully depicted by Khalil Gibran in his oft quoted poem: *The Garden of the Prophet* (1934).

'Pity the nation that is full of beliefs and empty of religion.

Pity the nation that raises not its voice when it walks in a funeral, boasts not except among its ruins, and will rebel not save when its neck is laid between the sword and the block.

Pity the nation whose statesman is a fox, whose philosopher is a juggler, and whose art is the art of patching and mimicking.

Pity the nation that welcomes to new ruler with trumpetings and farewells him with hootings, only to welcome another with trumpetings again.

Pity the nation whose sages are dumb with years and whose strong men are yet in the cradle.'

Such people deserve more of pity and compassion rather than anger and angst as they do not know what they are doing. They are incapable of using their own discretion. They can only receive order and obey. They don't know that revenge is against the true spirit of every religion. There is no difference between Hindu and Muslim fanaticism. Hence nobody is safe on account of such religious fanaticism.

Religious fanaticism of one group could not be countered by that of another religious group. We call India a great nation forgetting that a country comprising small men could never be great. Rama is the symbol of truth and high ideals of our country. Thus eulogizing murderous scene of Mahatma Gandhi is nothing short of killing the true spirit behind Rama and his ideals.

These religious fanatics failed to understand that Gandhi could not be destroyed this way. His ideas and philosophy may lie low for sometime but it would bounce back again at an appropriate time. That is the kind of seed Gandhi's ideas present. He is in the hearts and minds of the poor, homeless and dispossessed. He has got a permanent place there and could never be driven out from the popular mind. Even new interpretation of history denigrating Gandhi would not obliterate his role from the pages of history. But the real question is whether the good people are going to remain in deep slumber, leaving the entire field into the hands of bad people. As Abraham Lincoln put it: "To sin by silence when they should protest makes cowards of men." This is what exactly is happening at the moment to our country. Similar sentiments have been expressed by Martin Luther King Jr. when he said: "The ultimate tragedy is not the oppression and cruelty by the bad people but the silence over that by the good people." This is what is called silent support of the good people in the evil deeds of people with bad intentions. It is believed that the demons do not have their own powers. It is support of the good people which empowers them to perform evil deeds.

It is high time that we break our silence and actively participate in social life. There is a Gujrati saying that good people meet only at the cremation ground. If this goes on then Gandhi will be murdered day in and day out (*Contemplating Gandhi: Justice Chandrashekhar Dharmadhikari*, pp. 6-19).

8

Betrayal of Mahatma Gandhi

On August 14, 1947 India attained freedom from political bondage. Within a fortnight thereafter, an embittered patriot wrote to Gandhiji that so soon after the advent of freedom on the strength of precept and practice of *satya* and *ahimsa*, his followers had virtually started burying him alive. In a spirited reply, Gandhiji declared. "I cling to the hope that I have not yet been buried alive. The hope rests on the belief that the masses of India have not lost faith in the ideal. When it is proved that they too have lost it, the masses will suffer and they will be lost. Then, I can be said to be buried alive but so long as my faith burns bright, as I hope it will, even I stand alone, I shall be alive in my grave and, what is more, speaking from it."

India won freedom in a unique way, unparalleled in the annals of the world, through a civilized war without violence. Inspired and led by leader, who practised what he preached. A luminous symbol of sincerely and selflessness—Mohandas Karamchand Gandhi. He led the people and did not follow them cowardly for fear of losing illusory, ephemeral popularity.

During India's freedom struggle, Gandhi, the master transformed hundreds of thousands into "Indians first, Indians last and Indians always".

Today, where is India? Where are Indians? Of Gandhiji's dreams?

India is on the verge of ceasing to be the age-old, legendary Bharata Varsha, encompassing *Setu* (Rameshwaram) in the southern-most and Himalayas in the northern most tips of India—*Aasetu Himachala Paryantam.*

In today's India regional patriotism and linguistic fanaticism have practically submerged national patriotism and even human values. Our politics have become "pollutics". Corruptions—political, intellectual and monetary—has become a way of life with most people "Indians" have become rare biological specimens.

Alas! Our simple innocent people are sought to be de-Indianised by arousing parochial feelings and by fanning religious linguistic and regional hatreds. All this for petty transient political mileage.

What is the balance-sheet today? Has there been progress or retrogression? Has the objective of unity and solidarity been brought any nearer?

Alas! We have been steadily drilling towards disintegration. The governments, at the centre and in states, have looked askance at:

1. The plethora of regional and factional *senas*, all of which, under some specious plea, are allowed to carry on their divisive activities, without let or hindrance.
2. The spate of violent agitations on inter-state disputes relating to border, river water sharing, location of dams, steel plants, etc.
3. The series of subtle discriminatory orders. Rules and procedures via domicile regulations and the like, in the matter of employment, education, grants, loans, etc.

4. The continued selection of candidates for general elections, mid-term elections in some states, several by-elections to parliament and legislatures, municipal and panchayat elections, primarily on considerations of caste, religion and language.

Perhaps many leaders and ministers at the centre and in states feel that, if they soft-pedal in matters communal and more particularly regional and linguistic, their vote-catching potential will be ruined, that in the prevailing atmosphere, it is not real politik to denounce or deal firmly or completely shed "regional and linguistic patriotism."

Gandhiji wanted a Free India which will not tolerate

- Politics without principle!
- Wealth without Work
- Commerce without Morality
- Education without Character
- Pleasure without Conscience

Today's India, let us honestly confess, is fast coming to represent a negation of all the Values and the purity to public life for which Gandhiji stood.

Principled politics has become rare like desert blooms. The popular image of a politician is one who is unabashedly given to double-think and double-talk, quite contrary to Gandhi's dictum that there should be perfect accord of thought, word and deed.

Amassing wealth without any exertion has become the goal of, alas! A good many of our young men and even not-so-young men!

Today many are looking to the Stock Market for becoming instant rich, not realizing that abiding prosperity cannot via Stock Market, which can only lead to addiction to sleeping pills. There is no substitute for honest, hard, dedicated and unremitting toil.

The increase in the litigations that come up before the Consumer Redressal Fora is sufficient evidence of the thriving culture of commerce without morality.

As for education, a false interpretation of the concept of our secularism has taken away from our educational curriculum much of the religious, ethical and moral lessons devoted to character moulding.

Similarly, traditional restraints with regard to legitimate pleasures are all being cast to the winds. Power pelf and pleasure divorced from morality are having a field-day.

Gandhi gave us directions to follow not only in the political but in the social, economic and religious fields as well so that the national marches along with its Standard of Life raised side by side with the Standard of Living. Village uplift and rural regeneration formed the cornerstone of his economic thinking.

The present decline in the standards of public morality has been conspicuously step. We may have no answer to posterity if it asks: "Why did you allow the country to slip from that standard that Gandhi set for it for all time."

The general run of our present day "practicing politician" who masquerade as "servants of the people" so live in the sensation of self-seeking that their personality has almost run to seed. As men, most of them care only for themselves and can read only their news in headlines.

Our present-day politicians have almost desecrated our sacred Temple of Freedom built by Godmen, like Gandhi and other great torch-bearers nurtured in ethical and spiritual values, with the blood, sweat, toil and tears of millions of unknown patriots.

With the modern politicians, posture of half unworldly saintliness and preventions selfless service, these penchant for deliberate evasion and vagueness, fidgeting and fuming expletives, idiosyncrasies and eccentricities expletives, artful dodging and shameless self-seeking their crudely cultivated habit of making statements and taking actions which very seldom, if at all, respond to the test of accuracy and truth, the silken fabric of India's public life woven with the warp and woof of *satya* (truth). *Ahimsa* (non-violence), *asteya* (non-possession), *aparigraha* (non-covetousness) has been soiled, defiled, nay, torn to-pieces.

Naked force, coupled with cunning and fraud, unscrupulous, unholy, hotchpotch, alliances with unprincipled factions and groups and false promises and unabashed alibis to hoodwink the masses have become the main methods of capturing and clinging to power.

The creed of the majority of our politicians has become disturbance is the best way to peace, hatred to love, and fraud to sincerity, vilification and vindictiveness are shortcuts to power-grab and power-retention. Who then will guard the guardians *Quis custodiet ipsos custodes*?

The ideal of "Government of the people, by the people and for the people" has degenerated into "Government *off* the people, *buy* the people and *far* the people". Indeed, we have now "Government of the politicians, by the politicians and for the politicians."

Another disquieting factor in that but with rare exception, the qualification for leadership of most of the ruling politicians today consist in their capacity or adroitness for machinations, manipulations and manoeuvres; skill in fanning lower human emotions and subordinate loyalties for the promotion of their personal ambitions, cleverness in the art of making or collecting money and patronage by all possible means in utter disregard of ethical or moral norms, often exploiting position and power in the process; and a talent for diplomatic hypocrisy and sincere lying—double think and double—talk.

It is a pity that, noble as most of the present-day politicians may be as individuals, when they function as representatives of powerful political cliques, they succumb to perfidious and nihilistic tendencies and, by and large, become conscious or unconscious tools of frauds and foul play in the unholy game of naked power politics, designed to retain or wrest power for themselves or, at best, for their party.

A still more baneful element, corroding our national life, is aggressive linguism or 'regional patriotism'.

Politics has reached a blind alley. It moves in singular direction, i.e. politics and still more politics. In the arena of politics, even social service is primarily motivated by power considerations and not vice versa, service for power and not power for social service. What is worse, party politics, marked by casteism, religion and regionalism, has become the prime mover in the field of social service. Every political person could be seen asserting with a sense of pride that he or his wife is selflessly engaged in some kind of social work. His visiting card would bear a clear testimony for it. In fact, under the hypocritical garb of social service, such people unabashedly pursue their political interests only. A similar drive has also entered into the religious and social service fields, polluting these areas in the process. Thus social service and religious works are not only being politicised but they are also being commercialized. Their real values are being diminished but their market prices are on the ascent. In this context, one is reminded of Oscar Wilde's oft-quoted statement: 'Cynic is a person who knows the price of everything and value of nothing.' Social and moral values are being replaced by the market values. Social institutions are also being used for securing power positions and all the ills of power politics have entered into the arena of social service in a big way. Search for power positions and its concomitant electoral politics have become the order of the day even in social and religious institutions like temples, orphanage, old age home, blind schools and in similar other institutions. Elections in these institutions are held to garner and grab power positions. Thus, even the centres of social service have come under the game of power politics.

It is a real tragedy of our time that in every field good people remain indifferent and passive; whereas bad elements are ruling the roost. As a result, power and wealth are dominating all areas of human concerns. Hence cut-throat competition and cooperation is becoming the order of the day.

Today everything is on sale such as science, honesty, knowledge, nay, even man and God are there for sale. There is hardly anything which could not be bought and sold in the market. In a market, dominated with a price tag on everything, where is the place for the value of things! Gandhi's emphasis was on the value of things and not their prices. He even tried to base his social and economic thinking on such a worldview; Mammon is demon was his basic promise. Now the meaning and interpretations of morality and immorality has completely changed. Corruption has become the way of life. The entire market has been turned into a kind of black market. Fair market has virtually become non-existent. There was a time when in every shop there used to be placard saying honesty is the best policy. Now honesty has ceased to be the principle, it has been turned into a policy. And this kind of policy only means that untruth should be presented as truth putting on it false and attractive clothing. How could be there any place for honesty and moral and upright persons in such a market. In such an environment of loot and dishonesty; why one should fear and respect Gandhi?

Now a facsimile of Gandhi is put on the currency notes. Thus notes ranging from ₹ five to ₹ one thousand are judged only on the basis of their market price. Currency notes are medium of exchange and as such they carry only exchange value otherwise they are just pieces of paper. Gandhi is there on the stamps of the post office and he is stamped with a kind of big bang. Currency notes are kept in the lockers of banks as a part of black money. Now currency notes bearing Gandhi's facsimile are not merely medium of exchange, but even men and women are being bought and sold through them. They are also being used to buy votes during election times. Men and women have become marketable commodities as they are openly bought and sold in the market. Bad currency drives out the good currency, one of the basic principles of economics has started covering every walk of our life including our social, political and religious lives. Now Gandhi has been uprooted from every arena of our national life. To banish Gandhi from all walks of our lives, he is placed in statues made of marble and metal alleys. He is also to be found in musical and devotional songs on television and other audio-visual systems. His life and thoughts are being discussed and debated by the people who neither wear *Khadi nor* understand the value of *swadeshi*. Munnabhai's Gandhigiri is becoming more popular than Gandhi himself. Gandhi's picture is hung in the government offices. But it is mostly put on the wall behind the working tables of officers so that Gandhi does not see their acts of bribery. The real importance is given to the man sitting in the front and occasionally he also takes the name of Gandhi. Now *Vaishnav Jan* (the man of God) is not one who empathises with the suffering people (*pirparaijane*) but one who victimises helpless and hapless people. Even honouring Gandhi on certain ceremonial occasions is done more as a matter of ritual rather than out of genuine respect.

Gandhi is permanently placed and confined to his Samadhi, far away from the day-to-day life of our people. Why one should be scared of such a lifeless Gandhi! One could sum up the entire scenario in the words of a Hindi poet, as follows:

> 'Flowers I have offered
> On the dead body of the man
> He has also been murdered
> At my instance'

This is fully true of Gandhi and his place in our national life. He has just become a figure of ritualistic worship. Gandhi is totally driven out of our social and national life. He is dead along with his thoughts! That is the real tragedy of our national life (*Contemplating Gandhi: Justice Chandrashekhar Dharmadhikari*, pp. 201-02 & 274-76).

Dr. Aloo J. Dastur, in her article to "Mahatma Gandhi-Sole Hope and Alternative" edited by me writes: "Non-violence, non-cooperation, passive resistance, civil disobedience and fast were progressively chiseled and moulded by him for use at different times and under different circumstances. In Today's India, fasting rather its caricature, is common. The purpose for the fast is not of a serious or high order. It is pressure tactics. Travesty of another Gandhian technique is the Yatra, pad yatra from Kanyakumari to Kashmir, Rath Yatras and the Rath's cheap imitations of Raths of glorified ancient times.

Seventy-five years after Gandhiji's death, there is a little of Gandhian ideal. He rests in history books and on pedestal, not in the hearts and minds and souls of people. There is hardly anything of him except hearing one or two of his pronouncements on All India Radio or Doordarshan, seeing his face on postage stamps and currency notes or many statues of him springing all over the country or that many streets bear his name. Virtually every town and city in India has statue of Gandhiji. How did Gandhiji respond when the idea of a statue of him being erected in Mumbai was proposed in 1947. He said:

> "I must descent emphatically from any proposal to spend any money on preparing a statue of me, especially at a time when people do not have enough food and clothing. In Bombay the beautiful in-sanitation reign. There is so much overcrowding, that poor people are packed like sardines. Wise use of ten lakhs of rupees will consist in its being spent on some public utility. That would be the best statue." Gandhiji would happily forsake a thousand statues of himself for one man or woman or even a child who attempted to live according to his principles. The last thing that he wanted was to be put on pedestal and worshipped.

Every successive government, although none was strictly speaking Gandhian, have been chanting the mantra: "We have to go the Gandhian way. The political parties, particularly the Congress have continued to perceive the benefit to using Gandhiji to further their designs. They know that if they do not speak of Gandhiji and Gandhism to masses they will be thrown out of power. Jayaprakash Narayan, once stated that the Congress party presented itself for propaganda purposes as the Gandhi party, but it completely neglected his teachings."

Justice M.C. Chagla, who was Chief Justice of Bombay High Court and Union Minister has said: "There is hardly a platform where Gandhiji's name is not uttered very often in vain. The most dishonest, the most disreputable and the most corrupt politicians capitalize on his name and everyday he is being assassinated again not in the body, but in the spirit."

The sad thing is that Gandhiji as he was, has not reached the younger generation. Only the distorted Gandhi has reached them. Some thoughts of Gandhiji have reached the younger generation through his followers who have been too much engaged in politics. At times the younger generation has known Gandhiji through those persons who followed him with complete honesty until independence was attained and subsequently with equal dishonesty deserted him. They kept on encashing Gandhiji and garlanding his statues. Further more, his followers did him injustice by being too rigid and not allowing the slightest modifications of the classical Gandhian thought.

Those who ask others to follow the path shown by Gandhiji without themselves doing anything of the kind constitute a class by themselves. I classify Gandhians in three categories: Hypocrite Gandhians; so-called Gandhians and true Gandhians. There is no dearth of hypocrite Gandhians. The sole purpose of their life is to thrive on Gandhiji's name, killing his spirit every moment. The so-called Gandhians think that they have alone understood Gandhiji and they alone can make him understand to others. The true Gandhians are the ones who are carrying the legacy of Gandhiji, but their number is too small.

Dr. Zakir Hussain, who was President of India had said: "The new generation does not know Gandhi and more may not know him unless you make him known. Gandhi is very much in the background. If you bring him to their notice and make them love him, have regard for him for the things he said, you would have done a great deal."

Frankly speaking, it is not only the younger generation to whom Gandhiji has to be introduced. The Father of the Nation is needed to be re-introduced to the older generation also. They have almost forgotten him and have started talking and behaving just contrary to what Gandhiji preached and followed. Today, Gandhiji has been made object of ritual worship at annual birth and death anniversaries.

Every year on Gandhiji's birth and death anniversary, we pay lip sympathy to him. He is then forgotten for the rest of the year. His name is quite often mentioned in reverence as one mentions the name of a saint or a prophet, but Gandhian activities are dying with a whimper all over the country. The gulf between the India of Gandhiji's dreams and the designs of the government for the development is growing wider and wider. Gandhi caps and Khadi continue to be worn, but they are no longer the livery of freedom fighters and patriots and a symbol of devotion, dedication and honesty. Khadi has become a symbol of utter dishonesty and people look at it with contempt. The Khadi idea as Gandhiji propagated is dead. This is evident from the European dress, the Congress ministers and Congress leaders wear.

When Parliament Ignored Mahatma Gandhi

Inder Jit, Journalist M.P., in his article wrote:

> "Acharya Kripalani was ever so right. Speaking in the Lok Sabha, some 25 years ago, he called us Indians the "World's most sanctimonious humbugs" and added

> "We call a person the Father of the Nation. Yet, we do not mind his being insulted after his death." The provocation? A book by Ritwik Ghatak, in which he made uncharitable references to Gandhi. The Acharya wanted the book banned. But nothing came of his effort. Instead, Ghatak was given a Republic Da Award. Indira Gandhi was then the Prime Minister and V.V. Giri the President."

He further writes:

> "These thoughts are prompted by another scandalous happening, which has largely escaped the attention of both the public and the media. It relates to Parliament's special session on 50th Anniversary of Independence to commemorate the Golden Jubilee of India's 'SWARAJ'. Outwardly, everything went off well. A record number of members participated in it. The Speaker of the Lok Sabha, Purno Sangma made history by initiating the discussion. At the end, he moved a resolution from the chair which was voted unanimously. An identical resolution was also adopted unanimously by the Rajya Sabha.
>
> "Appropriately, the resolution "Remembered with gratitude the great sacrifices made and the salutary service rendered by our freedom fighters." It also "recalled with deep satisfaction and pride the maturity of our people in vigilantly preserving Democracy and safeguarding the Unity of the Nation." It then proceeded to solemnly affirm Our joint and unanimous commitment to an Agenda for India."
>
> "Shockingly, however, the resolution failed to refer to Mahatma Gandhi even once or to his programme for social and economic transformation. I was intrigued by the absence of Gandhi's name, as I listened to Speaker Sangma read out the resolution. Omission of his name in a resolution commemorating 50 years of freedom seemed impossible. I thought that perhaps, the poor

> quality of the earphones had played a trick. But I was soon face to face with the bitter truth. Gandhi's name was just not there in an official release of the resolution.

No one has any credible explanation for what came to pass. Even senior MP's and top leaders are to this day unaware of the slip-up. They blame it on their leaders pleading. "We had left it to them to finalise the resolution. They should not have slipped up. We need hang our heads in shame...." Enquiries show that the Lok Sabha Speaker initially invited all the leaders to suggest inputs for the resolution. A resolution was thereupon drafted and then vetted by the top leaders of all the major political parties, senior Ministers and Prime Minister Gujral himself. Finally, it was okayed by Speaker Sangma and the Rajya Sabha Chairman Krishna Kant (*Inder Jit, Journalist M.P.: Gandhians In Action,* Vols. IV and V, 1997-1998, Edited by Jitendra Singh, pp. 157-58).

9

India of Mahatma Gandhi's Dreams

Mahatma Gandhi in his writings in *Harijan*, *Young India* and *Hind Swaraj* expressed his views on India of his dreams, which are reproduced below:

> I shall work for an India, in which the poorest shall feel that it is their country in whose making they have an effective voice; in which there shall be no high class and low class of people; an India in which all communities shall live in perfect harmony. There can be no room in such an India for the curse of untouchability or the curse of the intoxicating drinks and drugs. Women will enjoy the same rights as men. Since we shall be at peace with all the rest of the world, neither exploiting, nor being exploited, we should have the smallest army imaginable. All interests not in conflict with the interests of the dumb millions will be scrupulously respected, whether foreign or indigenous. Personally, I hate distinction between foreign and indigenous. This is the India of my dreams.
>
> ...I shall be satisfied with nothing less.

Young India, 10-9-'31

The Swaraj of my dream is the poor man's Swaraj. The necessaries of life should be enjoyed by you in common with those enjoyed by the princes and the moneyed men. But that does not mean that you should have palaces like theirs. They are not necessary for happiness. You or I would be lost in them. But you ought to get all the ordinary amenities of life that a rich man enjoys. I have not the slightest doubt that Swaraj is not Poorna Swaraj until these amenities are guaranteed to you under it.

Young India, 26-3-'31

Let there be no mistake about my conception of Swaraj. It is complete independence of alien control and complete economic independence. So at one end you have political independence, at the other the economic. It has two other ends. One of them is moral and social the corresponding end is Dharma, i.e. religion in the highest sense of the term. It includes Hinduism, Islam, Christianity, etc., but is superior to them all.... Let us call this the square of Swaraj, which will be out of shape if any of its angles is untrue.

Harijan, 2-1-'37

The Swaraj of my conception will come only when all of us are firmly persuaded that our Swaraj has got to be won, worked and maintained through truth and Ahimsa alone. True democracy or Swaraj of the masses can never come through untruthful and violent means, for the simple reason that the natural corollary to their use would be to remove all opposition through the suppression or extermination of the antagonists. That does not make for individual freedom. Individual freedom can have the fullest play only under a regime of unadulterated Ahimsa.

Harijan, 27-5-'39

In Swaraj based on Ahimsa people need not know their rights, but it is necessary for them to know their duties. There is no duty but creates a corresponding right, and those only are true rights which flow from a due performance of one's duties. Hence rights of citizenship accrue only to those who serve the State to which they belong. And they alone can do justice to the rights that accrue to them. Everyone possesses the right to tell lies or resort to goondaism. But the exercise of such a right is harmful both to the exerciser and society. But to him who observes truth and non-violence comes prestige, and prestige brings rights. And people who obtain rights as a result of performance of duty, exercise them only for the service of society, never for themselves. Swaraj of a people means the sum total of the Swaraj (self-rule) of individuals. And such Swaraj comes only from performance by individuals of their duty as citizens. In it no one thinks of his rights. They come, when they are needed, for better performance of duty.

Harijan, 25-3-'39

Under Swaraj based on non-violence nobody is anybody's enemy, everybody contributes his or her due quota to the common goal, all can read and write, and their knowledge keeps growing from day to day. Sickness and disease are reduced to the minimum. No one is a pauper and labour can always find employment. There is no place under such a government for gambling, drinking and immorality or for class hatred. The rich will use their riches wisely and usefully, and not squander them in increasing their pomp and worldly pleasures. It should not happen that a handful of rich people should live in jewelled palaces and the millions in miserable hovels devoid of sunlight or ventilation. In non-violent Swaraj there can be no encroachment upon just rights; contrariwise no one can possess unjust rights. In a well-organized State, usurpation should be an impossibility and it should be unnecessary to resort to force for dispossessing an usurper.

Harijan, 25-3-'39

THE CURSE OF INDUSTRIALISM

There is a growing body of enlightened opinion which distrusts this civilization which has insatiable material ambition at one end and consequent war at the other. But whether good or bad, why must India become industrial in the Western sense? The Western civilization is urban. Small countries like England or Italy may afford to urbanize their systems. A big country like America with a very sparse population, perhaps, cannot do otherwise. But one would think that a big country with a teeming population with an ancient rural tradition which has hitherto answered its purpose, need not, must not copy the Western model. What is good for one nation situated in one condition is not necessarily good enough for another differently situated. One man's food is often another man's poison. Physical geography of a country has a predominant share in determining its culture. A fur coat may be necessity for the dweller in the polar regions, it will smother those living in the equatorial regions.

Young India, 25-7-'29

I would categorically state my conviction that the mania for mass-production is responsible for the world crisis. Granting for the moment that machinery may supply all the needs of humanity, still, it would concentrate production, in particular areas, so that you would have to go about in a round about way to regulate distribution; whereas, if there is production and distribution both in the respective areas where things are required, it is automatically regulated, and there is less chance for fraud, none for speculation.

You see that these nations (Europe and America) are able to exploit the so-called weaker or unorganized races of the world. Once these races gain an elementary knowledge and decide that they are no more going to be exploited, they will simply be satisfied with what they can provide themselves. Mass-production, then at least where the vital necessities are concerned, will disappear.

When production and consumption both become localized, the temptation to speed up production, indefinitely and at any price, disappears. All the endless difficulties and problems that our present-day economic system presents, too, would then come to an end.

Harijan, 2-11-'34

Machinery has its place; it has come to stay. But it must not be allowed to displace necessary human labour. I would welcome every improvement in the cottage machine, but I know that it is criminal to displace hand labour by the introduction of power-driven spindles unless one is at the same time ready to give millions of farmers some other occupation in their houses.

Young India, 5-11-'25

I refuse to be dazzled by the seeming triumph of machinery. I am uncompromisingly against all destructive machinery. But simple tools and instruments and such machinery as saves individual labour and lightens the burden of the millions of cottages, I should welcome.

Young India, 17-6-'26

Dead machinery must not be pitted against the millions of living machines represented by the villagers scattered in the seven hundred thousand villages of India. Machinery to be well used has to help and ease human effort. The present use of machinery tends more and more to concentrate wealth in the hands of a few in total disregard of millions of men and women whose bread is snatched by it out of their mouths.

Harijan, 14-9-'35

Industrialization on a mass scale will necessarily lead to passive or active exploitation of the villagers as the problems of competition and marketing come in. Therefore, we have to concentrate on the village being self-contained, manufacturing mainly for use. Provided this character of the industry is maintained, there would be no objection to villagers using even the modern machines and tools that they can make and can afford to use. Only they should not be used as a means of exploitation of others.

Harijan, 29-8-'36

I do not believe that industrialization is necessary in any case for any country. It is much less so for India. Indeed, I believe that Independent India can only discharge her duty towards a groaning world by adopting a simple but ennobled life by developing her thousands of cottages and living at peace with the world. High thinking is inconsistent with complicated material life based on high speed imposed on us by Mammon worship. All the graces of life are possible only when we learn the art of living nobly.

There may be sensation in living dangerously. We must draw the distinction between living in the face of danger and living dangerously. A man who dares to live alone in a forest infested by wild beasts and wilder men without a gun and with God as his only Help, lives in the face of danger. A man who lives perpetually in mid-air and dives to the earth below to the admiration of a gaping world lives dangerously. One is a purposeful, the other a purposeless life.

Whether such plain living is possible for an isolated nation, however large geographically and numerically in the face of a world, armed to the teeth, and in the midst of pomp and circumstance, is a question open to the doubt of a sceptic. The answer is straight and simple. If plain life is worth living, then the attempt is worth making, even though only an individual or a group makes the effort.

At the same time I believe that some key industries are necessary. I do not believe in armchair or armed socialism. I believe in action according to my belief, without waiting for wholesale conversion. Hence, without having to enumerate key industries, I would have State ownership, where a large number of people have to work together. The ownership of the products of their labour, whether skilled or unskilled, will vest in them through the State. But as I can conceive such a state only based on non-violence, I would not dispossess moneyed men by force but would invite their co-operation in to process of conversion to state ownership. There are no pariahs of society, whether they are millionaires or paupers. The two are sores of the same disease.

And I avow this belief in the face of the inhumanities we have witnessed and may still have to witness in India as elsewhere. Let us live in the face of danger.

Harijan, 1-9-'46

THE PROBLEM OF UNEMPLOYMENT

We should be ashamed of resting or having a square meal so long as there is one able-bodied man or woman without work or food.

Young India, 6-10-'21

Imagine a nation working only five hours per day on an average, and this not by choice but by force of circumstances, and you have a realistic picture of India. If the reader would visualize the picture, he must dismiss from his mind the busy fuss of the city life or the grinding fatigue of the factory life or the slavery of the plantation. These are but drops in the ocean of Indian humanity. If he would visualize the picture of the Indian skeleton, he must think of the eighty per cent of the population which is working its own fields, and which has practically no occupation for at least four months in the year, and which therefore lives on the borderland of starvation. This is the normal condition. The ever recurring famines make a large addition to this enforced idleness.

Young India, 3-11-'21

The reason why our average life-rate is deplorably low, the reason why we are getting more and more impoverished is that we have neglected our 7,00,000 villages. We have indeed thought of them, but only to the extent of exploiting them. We read thrilling accounts of the 'glory that was Ind', and of the land that was flowing with milk and honey; but today it is a land of starving millions. We are sitting in this fine pandal under a blaze of electric lights, but we do not know that we are burning these lights at the expense of the poor. We have no right to use these lights if we forget that we owe these to them.

There is a difference between the civilization of the East—the civilization of India and that of the West. It is not generally realized wherein the difference lies. Our geography is different, our history is different, our ways of living are different. Our continent, though vast, is a speck of the globe, but it is the most thickly populated, barring China. Well, now, the economics and civilization of a country where the pressure of population on land is greatest are and must be different from those of a country where the pressure is least. Sparsely populated, America may have need of machinery. India may not need it at all. Where there are millions of units of idle labour, it is no use thinking of labour-saving devices. If someone devised a machine which saved us the trouble of using our hands to eat, eating would cease to be a pleasure, it would become a torture. The reason of our poverty is the extinction of our industries and our consequent unemployment. Some years ago India's agricultural population was said to be 70 per cent. Today it is said to be 90 per cent. It does not mean that 90 per cent are agriculturists, but that, instead of 70 per cent who depended on land, 90 per cent are now driven to depend on land. In other words, whereas there were industries and crafts enough to feed the 20 per cent, some time ago, these are no longer there and the people have thus been thrown on land. They thus steal their living, not because they want to, but because there is no more land.

Not that there is not enough land to feed our 35 crores. It is absurd to say that India is over populated and that the surplus population must die. I am sure that if all the land that is available was properly utilized and made to yield up to its capacity, it would surely maintain the whole population. Only we have got to be industrious and to make two blades of grass grow where one grows today.

The remedy is to identify ourselves with the poor villager and to help him make the land yield its plenty, help him produce what we need, and confine ourselves to use what he produces, live as he lives, and persuade him to take to more rational ways of diet and living.

We eat mill-ground flour, and even the poor villager walks with a head-load of half a maund grain to have it ground in the nearest flour mill. Do you know that in spite of the plenty of foodstuffs we produce we import wheat from outside and we eat the superfine flour from Australia? We will not use our hand-ground flour, and the poor villager also foolishly copies us. We thus turn our wealth into waste, nectar into poison. For whole meal is the proper meal. Mill-ground flour is vitaminless flour, mill-ground flour kept for days is not only vitaminless, but poison. But we will not exert ourselves to produce flour which we must eat fresh every day, and will pay for less nutritious things and purchase ill-health in the bargain. This is not any abstruse economic truth, it is a fact which is daily happening before our eyes. The same is the case with rice and gur and oil. We will eat rice, polished of its substance, and eat less nutritious sugar and pay more for it than more nutritious gur. We have suffered the village oilman to be driven to extinction and we eat adulterated oils. We idolize the cow, but kill her by slow degrees. We eat honey and kill the honey-bee, with the result that honey is such a rare commodity today that it is only available to a Mahatma like me or to those who must have it from the physician as a vehicle for the drugs he prescribes. If we took the trouble of learning scientific and harmless bee-keeping, we should get it cheaper and our children would get out of it all the carbohydrates, they need. In all our dietetics we mistake the shadow for the substance, preferring bone-white sugar to rich brown gur and pale white bread to rich brown bran-bread.

Harijan, 11-5-'30

In one sense the problem of unemployment in our country is not so difficult as in other countries. The mode of life is a great factor. The Western unemployed worker must have warm clothing, boots or shoes and socks like the rest of the people, he must have a warm house and many other things incidental to the cold climate. We do not want all these things. I have indeed wept to see the stark poverty and unemployment in our country, but I must confess our own negligence and ignorance are responsible for it. We do not know the dignity of labour as such. Thus a shoe-maker will not do anything beyond his shoes, he will think all other labour is below his dignity. That wrong notion must go. There is enough employment in India for all who will work with their hands and feet honestly. God has given everyone the capacity to work and earn more than his daily bread and whoever is ready to use that capacity is sure to find work. No labour is too mean for one who wants to earn an honest penny. The only thing is the readiness to use the hands and feet that God has given us.

Harijan, 19-12-'36

We are either ignorant or negligent of the divine law by virtue of which man has been given only his daily bread and no more, with the result that there arise inequalities with all the misery attendant upon them. The rich have a superfluous store of things which they do not need and which are, therefore, neglected and wasted; while millions starve and are frozen to death for want of them. If each retained possession only of what he needed, no one would be in want and all would live in contentment. As it is, the rich are discontented no less than the poor. The poor man would become a millionaire and the millionaire a multi-millionaire. The poor are often not satisfied when they get just enough to fill their stomachs; but they are clearly entitled to it and society should make it a point to see they get it. The rich must take an initiative in the matter with a view to a universal diffusion of the spirit of contentment. If only they keep their own property within moderate limits the poor will be easily fed, and will learn the lesson of contentment along with rich.

From Yeravda Mandir, Chap. VI

Civilization in the real sense of the term consists not in the multiplication but in the deliberate and voluntary reduction of wants, which promotes real happiness and contentment and increases the capacity for service. One can reduce one's wants by perseverance, and the reduction of wants makes for happiness—a healthy body and a peaceful mind.

From Yeravda Mandir, Chap. VI

The golden rule...is resolutely to refuse to have what millions cannot. This ability to refuse will not descend upon us all of a sudden. The first thing is to cultivate the mental attitude that will not have possessions or facilities denied to millions, and the next immediate thing is to re-arrange our lives as fast as possible in accordance with that mentality.

Young India, 24-6-'26

Jesus, Muhammed, Buddha, Nanak, Kabir, Chaitanya, Shankara, Dayanand, Ramakrishna were men who exercised an immense influence over and moulded the character of thousands of men. The world is the richer for their having lived in it. And they were all men who deliberately embraced poverty as their lot.

Speeches and Writings of Mahatma Gandhi, p. 353

What India needs is not the concentration of capital in a few hands, but its distribution so as to be within easy reach of the 7, lakhs of villages that make this continent 1900 miles long and 1500 miles broad.

Young India, 23-3-'21

VILLAGE SANITATION

Divorce between intelligence and labour has resulted in criminal negligence of the villages. And so, instead of having graceful hamlets dotting the land, we have dung heaps. The approach to many villages is not a refreshing experience. Often one would like to shut one's eyes and stuff one's nose; such is the surrounding dirt and offending smell. A sense of national or social sanitation is not a virtue among us. We may take a kind of a bath, but we do not mind dirtying the well or the tank or the river by whose side or in which we perform ablutions. I regard this defect as a great vice which is responsible for the disgraceful state of our villages and the sacred banks of the sacred rivers and for the diseases that spring from insanitation.

Lanes and streets have to be cleansed of all the rubbish, which should be classified. There are portions which can be turned into manure, portions which have simply to be buried and portions which can be directly turned into wealth. Every bone picked up is valuable raw material from which useful articles can be made or which can be crushed into rich manure. Rags and waste-paper can be turned into paper, and excreta picked up are golden manure for the village fields. At present, this rich manure, valued at lakhs of rupees, runs to waste every day, fouls the air and brings disease into the bargain.

Village tanks are promiscuously used for bathing, washing clothes, and drinking and cooking purposes. Many village tanks are also used by cattle. Buffaloes are often to be seen wallowing in them.

An ideal Indian village will be so constructed as to lend itself to perfect sanitation. It will have cottages with sufficient light and ventilation built of a material obtainable within a radius of five miles of it. The cottages will have courtyards enabling householders to plant vegetables for domestic use and to house their cattle. The village lanes and streets will be free of all avoidable dust. It will have wells according to its needs and accessible to all. It will have houses of worship for all, also a common meeting place, a village common for grazing its cattle, a co-operative dairy, primary and secondary schools in which industrial education will be the central fact, and it will have Panchayats for settling disputes. It will produce its own grains, vegetables and fruit, and its own Khadi. This is roughly my idea of a model village. There are in our villages inexhaustible resources not for commercial purposes in every case but certainly for local purposes in almost every case. The greatest tragedy is the hopeless unwillingness of the villagers to better their lot.

Harijan, 9-1-'37

VILLAGE HEALTH

I hold that where the rules of personal, domestic and public sanitation are strictly observed and due care is taken in the matter of diet and exercise, there should be no occasion for illness or disease. Where there is absolute purity, inner and outer, illness becomes impossible. If the village people could but understand this, they would not need doctors, hakims or vaidyas.

Harijan, 26-5-'46

Nature cure implies an ideal mode of life and that in its turn presupposes ideal living conditions in towns and villages. The name of God is, of course, the hub round which the nature cure system revolves.

Nature cure implies that the treatment should be the cheapest and the simplest possible. The ideal is that such treatment should be carried out in the villages. The villagers should be able to provide the necessary means and equipment. What cannot be had in the villages should be procured. Nature cure does mean a change for the better in one's outlook on life itself. It means regulation of one's life in accordance with the laws of health. It is not a matter of taking the free medicine from the hospital or for fees. A man who takes free treatment from the hospital accepts charity. The man who accepts nature cure never begs. Self-help enhances self-respect. He takes steps to cure himself by eliminating poisons from the system and takes precautions against falling ill in the future.

Right diet and balanced diet are necessary. Today our villages are as bankrupt as we are ourselves. To produce enough vegetables, fruits and milk in the villages, is an essential part of the nature cure scheme.

Time spent on this should not be considered a waste. It is bound to benefit all the villagers and ultimately the whole of India.

Harijan, 2-6-'46

The man who its to live, who is friends with the five power, earth, water, ether, sun and air and who is a servant of God, the Creator of all these, ought not to fall ill. If he does, he will remain calm relying on God and die in peace, if need be. If there are any medicinal herbs in the fields of his village he may make use of them. Doctors aver that 99% of disease springs from insanitation, from eating the wrong food and from under-nourishment. If we can teach this 99% the art of living, we can afford to forget the 1%.... Today pure water, good earth, fresh air, are unknown to us. We do not know the inestimable value of ether and the sun. If we make use of these five powers and if we eat the proper and balanced diet, we shall have done the work of ages. For acknowledging this knowledge, we need neither degrees nor crores of money. What we need are living faith in God, a zeal for service, an acquaintance with the five powers of nature and knowledge of dietetics. All this can be acquired without wasting time in schools and colleges.

Harijan, 1-9-'46

Disease springs from a willful or ignorant breach of the laws of nature. It follows, therefore, that timely return to those laws should mean restoration.

Harijan, 15-9-'46

I would like to know what the medical men and scientists are doing for the country. One finds them readily going to foreign lands to learn new modes of treating special diseases. I suggest that they should turn their attention towards the seven lakhs of the villages of India. They would immediately discover that all the qualified men and women are required for village service, not after the manner of the West but after the manner of the East. They will then adapt themselves to many indigenous systems. India does not need imported drugs from the West when she has an inexhaustible stock of a variety of drugs grown in the villages themselves. But more than drugs they have to teach the people the right mode of living.

Harijan, 15-6-'47

My nature cure is designed solely for villagers and villages. Therefore, there is no place in it for the microscope, X-rays and similar things. Nor is there room in nature cure for medicines, such as quinine, emetin and penicillin. Personal hygiene and healthy living are of primary importance. And these should suffice. If everyone could achieve perfection in this art, there could be no disease. And, while obeying all the laws of Nature in order to cure illness, if it does come, the sovereign remedy ever lies in Ramanama. But this cure through Ramanama cannot become universal in the twinkling of an eye. To carry conviction to the patient, the physician has to be a living embodiment of the power of Ramanama.

Harijan, 11-8-'46

URBAN SANITATION

The one thing which we can and must learn from the West is the science of municipal sanitation. The peoples of the West have evolved a science of corporate sanitation and hygiene from which we have much to learn. We must modify western methods of sanitation to suit our requirements.

Young India, 26-12-'24

Cleanliness is next to godliness. We can no more gain God's blessing with an unclean body than with an unclean mind. A clean body cannot reside in an unclean city.

Young India, 19-11-'25

No municipality can cope with insanitation and congestion by the simple process of taxation and paid services. This vital reform is possible only by wholesale and voluntary co-operation of the people both rich and poor.

Young India, 26-11-'25

In a village we may do many things with impunity but immediately we transfer ourselves to crowded streets where we have hardly air to breathe, the life becomes changed, and we have to obey another set of laws which immediately come into being. Do we do that? It is no use saddling the municipality with the responsibilities for the condition in which we find the central parts of every city in India, and I feel no municipality in the world will be able to over-ride the habits of a class of people handed to them from generation to generation. I, therefore, suggest that it is a question of sanitary reform in these big cities, which will be a hopeless task if we expect our municipalities to do this unaided by this voluntary work. Far be it from me to absolve the municipalities from their responsibilities.

Speeches and Writings of Mahatma Gandhi, pp. 375-76

I consider myself a lover of municipal life. I think that it is a rare privilege for a person to find himself in the position of a municipal councillor but let me note down for you as a man with some experience in public life that one indispensable condition of that privilege is that the municipal councillors dare not approach their office from interested or selfish motives. They must approach their sacred task in a spirit of service.

Young India, 28-3-'29

If I were a taxpayer within the jurisdiction of a local board or a municipality, I would refuse to pay a single pie by way of additional taxation and advise others to do likewise unless the money we pay is returned fourfold. Those who enter local boards and municipalities as representatives go there not to seek honour or to indulge in mutual rivalries, but to render a service of love and that does not depend upon money. Ours is a pauper country. If our municipal councillors are imbued with a real spirit of service, they will convert themselves into unpaid sweepers, bhangis and road-makers, and take pride in doing so. This means that a municipal councilor has to be a whole timer. He should have no axe of his own to grind.

Harijan, 18-2-'39

Leaving night-soil, cleaning the nose, or spitting on the road is a sin against God as well as humanity, and betrays a sad want of consideration for others. The man who does not cover his waste deserves a heavy penalty even if he lives in a forest.

Satyagraha in South Africa, p. 240

EVIL WROUGHT BY THE FOREIGN MEDIUM

To give millions knowledge of English is to enslave them. The foundation that Macaulay laid of education has enslaved us. I do not suggest that he had any such intention, but that has been the result. ...Is it not a painful thing that, if I want to go to a court of justice, I must employ the English language as a medium; that, when I become a Barrister, I may not speak my mother tongue, and that someone else should have to translate to me from my own language? Is not this absolutely absurd? Is it not a šign of slavery? Am I to blame the English for it or myself? It is we, the English knowing men, that have enslaved India. The curse of the nation will rest not upon the English but upon us.

Hind Swaraj, 1908

The strain of receiving instruction through a foreign medium is intolerable. Our children alone can bear it, but they have to pay for it. They become unfit to bear any other strain. For this graduates are mostly without stamina, weak, devoid of energy, diseased and mere imitators. Originality, research, adventure, ceaseless effort, courage, dauntlessness and such other qualities have become atrophies. We are thus incapacitated for undertaking new enterprises, and we are unable to carry them through if we undertake any. Some who can give proof of such qualities die an untimely death....

We the English-educated class are unfit to ascertain the true measure of the harm done by the unnatural system. We should get some idea of it if we realized how little we have reacted upon the masses.

The correspondence that should exist between the school training and the character imbibed with the mother's milk and the training received through her sweet speech is absent when the school training is given through a foreign tongue. However pure may be his motives, he who thus snaps the cord that should bind the school-life and the home-life is an enemy of the nation. We are traitors to our mothers by remaining under such a system. The harm done goes much further. A gulf has been created between the educated classes and the uneducated masses. The latter do not know us. We do not know the former. They consider us to be 'Saheblog'. They are afraid of us. They do not trust us. Fortunately, the educated class seems to be waking up from its trance. They experience the difficulty of contact with the masses. How can they infect the masses with their own enthusiasm for the national cause? They cannot do so through English.... Owing to the barrier thus created the flow of national life suffers impediment.

In fact is that when English occupies its proper place and the vernaculars receive their due, our minds which are today imprisoned will be set free and our brains though cultivated and trained, and yet being fresh, will not feel the weight of having to learn English as a language. And it is my belief that English thus learnt will be better than our English of today.

When we receive our education through the mother tongue, we should observe a different atmosphere in our homes. At present we are unable to make our wives co-partners with us. They know little of our activity. Our parents do not know what we learn. If we receive instruction through the mother tongue we should easily make our washer men, our barbers, and our bhangis, partakers of the high knowledge we might have gained. In England one discusses high politics with barbers while having a shave. We are unable to do so even in our family circle, not because the members of the family or the barbers are ignorant people. Their intellect is as well trained as that of the English barber. We are able to discuss intelligently with them the events of Mahabharat, Ramayana and of our holy places. For the national training flows in that direction. But we are unable to take home what we receive in our schools. We cannot reproduce before the family circle what we have learnt through the English language.

The greatest service we can render society is to free ourselves and it from the superstitious regard we have learnt to pay to the learning of the English language. It is the medium of instruction in our schools and colleges. It is becoming the lingua franca of the country. Our best thoughts are expressed in it.... This belief in the necessity of English training has enslaved us. It has unfitted us for true national service. Were it not for force of habit, we could not fail to see that by reason of English being the medium of instruction, our intellect has been segregated, we have been isolated from the masses, the best mind of the nation has become gagged and the masses have not received the benefit of the new ideas we have received. We have been engaged these past sixty years in memorizing strange words and their pronunciation instead of assimilating facts. In the place of building upon the foundation, training received from our parents, we have almost unlearnt it. There is no parallel to this in history. It is a national tragedy. The first and greatest Social Service we can render is to revert to vernaculars, to restore Hindi to its natural place as the National Language and begin carrying on all our provincial proceedings in our respective vernaculars and national proceedings in Hindi. We ought not to rest till our schools and colleges give us instruction through the vernaculars. ...The day must soon come when our legislatures will debate national affairs in the vernaculars or Hindi as the case may be. Hitherto the masses have been strangers to their proceedings. The vernacular papers have tried to undo the mischief a little. But the task was beyond them. The Patrika reserves its biting sarcasm, the Bengalee its learning, for ears tuned to English, in this ancient land of cultured thinkers the presence in our midst of a Tagore or a Bose or a Ray ought not to excite wonder. Yet the painful fact is that there are so few of them. From the presidential address to the First All India Social Service Conference held at Calcutta on 27th December 1917.

It is my considered opinion that English education in the manner it has been given has emasculated the English-educated Indian, it has put a severe strain upon the Indian students' nervous energy, and has made of us imitators. The process of displacing the vernacular has been one of the saddest chapters in the British connection.

Of all the superstitions that affect India, none is so great as that a knowledge of the English language is necessary for imbibing ideas of liberty, and developing accuracy of thought.

It was conceived and born in error, for the English rulers honestly believed the indigenous system to be worse than useless. It has been nurtured in sin, for the tendency has been to dwarf the Indian body, mind and soul.

Young India, 27-4-'21

Reply to Tagore

...English is today studied because of its commercial and so-called political value. Our boys think, and rightly in the present circumstances that without English they cannot get government as a passport to marriage. I know several instances of women wanting to learn English so that they may be able to talk to Englishmen in English. I know husbands who are sorry that their wives cannot talk to them and their friends in English. I know families in which English is being made the mother tongue. Hundreds of youth believe that without knowledge of English, freedom for India is practically impossible. The canker has so eaten into the society that in many cases, the only meaning of Education is knowledge of English. All these are for me signs of our slavery and degradation. It is unbearable to me that the vernaculars should be crushed and starved as they have been. I cannot tolerate the idea of parents writing to their children, or husbands writing to their wives, not in their vernaculars but in English. I hope I am as great a believer in free air as the great Poet. I do not want my house to be walled in on all sides and my windows to be stuffed. I want the cultures of all the lands to be blown about my house as freely as possible. But I refuse to be blown off my feet by any. I refuse to live in other peoples' houses as an interloper, a beggar or a slave. I refuse to put the necessary strain of learning English upon my sisters for the sake of false pride or questionable social advantage. I would have our young men and young women with literary tastes to learn as much English and other world languages as they like, and then expect them to give the benefits of their learning to India and to the world, like a Bose, a Roy or the Poet himself. But I would not have a single Indian to forget, neglect or be ashamed of his mother tongue, or to feel that he or she cannot think or express the best thoughts in his or her own vernacular. Mine is not a religion of the prison-house. It has room for the least among God's creation. But it is proof against insolence, pride of race, religion or colour.

Young India, 1-6-'21

The foreign medium has caused brain fag, put an undue strain upon the nerves of our children, made them crammers and imitators, unfitted them for original work and thought, and disabled them for filtrating their learning to the family or the masses. The foreign medium has made our children practically foreigners in their own land. It is the greatest tragedy of the existing system.

The foreign medium has prevented the growth of our vernaculars. If I had the powers of a despot, I would today stop the tuition of our boys and girls through a foreign medium, and require all the teachers and professors on pain of dismissal to introduce the change forthwith. I would not wait for the preparation of textbooks. They will follow the change. It is an evil that needs a summary remedy.

Young India, 1-9-'21

But for the fact that the only higher education, the only education worth the name has been received by us through the English medium, there would be no need to prove such a self-evident proposition that the youth of a nation to remain a nation must receive instruction including the highest in its own vernacular or vernaculars. Surely, it is a self-demonstrated position that the youth of a nation cannot keep or establish a living contact with the masses unless their knowledge is received and assimilated through a medium understood by the people. Who can calculate the immeasurable loss sustained by the nation owing to thousands of its young men having been obliged to waste years in mastering a foreign language and its idiom of which in their daily life they have the least use and in learning which they had to neglect their own mother tongue and their own literature? There never was a greater superstition than that a particular language can be incapable of expansion or expressing abstruse or scientific ideas. A language is an exact reflection of the character and growth of its speakers.

Among the many evils of foreign rule, this blighting imposition of a foreign medium upon the youth of the country will be counted by history as one of the greatest. It has sapped the energy of the nation, it has shortened the lives of the pupils. It has estranged them from the masses, it has made education unnecessarily expensive. If this process is still persisted in, it bids fair to rob the nation of its soul. The sooner, therefore, educated India shakes itself free from the hypnotic spell of the foreign medium, the better it would be for them and the people.

Young India, 5-7-'28

French writer and poet Romain Rolland played host to Mahatma Gandhi during his visit to Switzerland in December 1931. Rolland had earlier authored the book Mahatma Gandhi which discussed Gandhi's ideas at length. The two friends would spend hours together discussing important themes, including the worsening situation in Europe and the hope that lay in non-violence.

Mahatma Gandhi and Netaji Subhash Chandra Bose.

Father of our Nation is this holy war for India's liberation, we ask for your blessings and good wishes.

—Subhash Chandra Bose

I am not aching for martyrdom, but if it comes in my way in the prosecution of what I consider to be the supreme duty in defence of the faith I hold... I shall have earned it.

—M.K. Gandhi

Every moment of my life I realise that God is putting me on my trail.

—M.K. Gandhi

At Noakhali, East Bengal, 1946.

Mahatma Gandhi with Rabindranath Tagore, Shantiniketan, 1940.

He stopped at the threshold of the huts of the thousands of dispossessed, dressed like one of their own. He spoke to them in their own language. Here was living truth at last, and not only quotation from books. For this reason the Mahatma, the name given to him by the people of India, is his real name.

—Rabindranath Tagore

A meeting of the Congress Working Committee held in the library of Anand Bhavan, Allahabad, 1931.

(From left: Acharya Kripalani, Sardar Patel, Mahatma Gandhi and Vijaylakshmi Pandit).

My loin cloth is an organic evolution in my life. It came naturally without effort, without premediation.

—M.K. Gandhi

Overwhelming participation of women in the Quit India Movement, 1942.

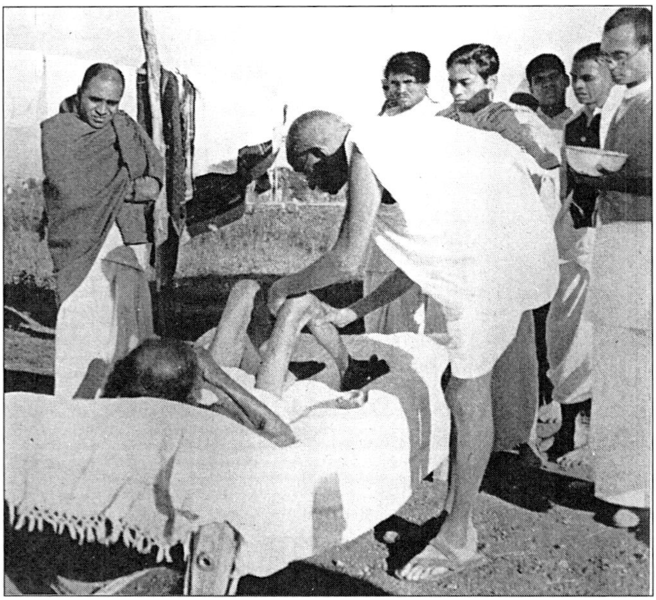

Mahatma Gandhi's daily attendance on a leprosy case, Segaon, 1939.

Addressing a mass meeting, Bengal, 1946.
I claim to know my millions. All the 24 hours of the day I am with them.
—M.K. Gandhi

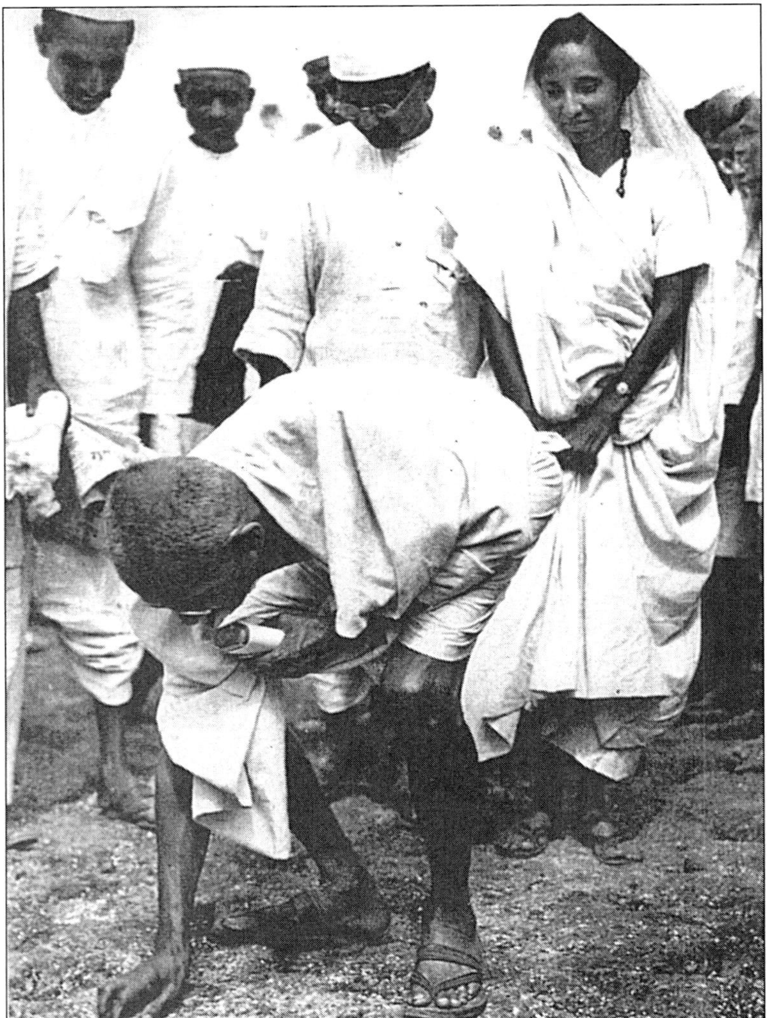

Dandi March: Salt Satyagraha, 12 March 1930.

No municipality can cope with insanitation and congestion by the simple process of taxation and paid services. This vital reform is possible only by wholesale voluntary co-operation of the people, both rich and poor.

—M.K. Gandhi

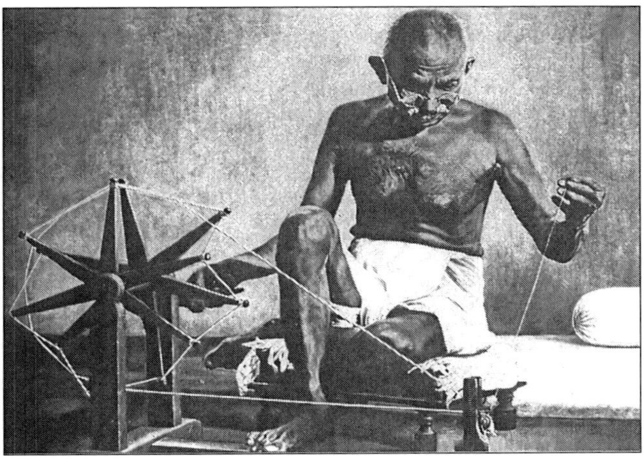

The Message of the spinning-wheel is much wider than its circumference. Its message is one of simplicity, service of mankind, living so as not to hurt others, creating an indissoluble bond between the rich and the poor, capital and labour, the prince and the peasant. The larger message is naturally for all.

—M.K. Gandhi

Mahatma's first meeting with Lord and Lady Mountbatten, Delhi, March 31, 1947.

I am not anti-English; I am not anti-British; I am not anti-any Government; but I am anti-untruth, anti-humbug, and anti-injustice. So long as the Government spells injustice, it may regard me as its enemy, implacable enemy.

No one will accuse me of any anti-English tendency. Indeed, I pride myself on my discrimination. I have thankfully copied many things from them. Punctuality, reticence, public hygiene, independent thinking and exercise of judgment and several other things I owe to my association with them.

—M.K. Gandhi

Index